D1601649

Restructuring for Integrative Education

Critical Studies in Education and Culture Series

Simulation, Spectacle, and the Ironies of Education Reform
Guy Senese with Ralph Page

Repositioning Feminism and Education: Perspectives on Educating for
Social Change
*Janice Jipson, Petra Munro, Susan Victor, Karen Froude Jones, and Gretchen
Freed-Rowland*

Culture, Politics, and Irish School Dropouts: Constructing Political
Identities
G. Honor Fagan

Anti-Racism, Feminism, and Critical Approaches to Education
Roxana Ng, Pat Staton, and Joyce Scane

Beyond Comfort Zones in Multiculturalism: Confronting the Politics of
Privilege
Sandra Jackson and José Solís, editors

Culture and Difference: Critical Perspectives on the Bicultural
Experience in the United States
Antonia Darder

Poststructuralism, Politics and Education
Michael Peters

Weaving a Tapestry of Resistance: The Places, Power, and Poetry of a
Sustainable Society
Sharon Sutton

Counselor Education for the Twenty-First Century
Susan J. Brotherton

Positioning Subjects: Psychoanalysis and Critical Educational Studies
Stephen Appel

Adult Students "At-Risk": Culture Bias in Higher Education
Timothy William Quinnan

Education and the Postmodern Condition
Michael Peters, editor

Restructuring for Integrative Education

Multiple Perspectives, Multiple Contexts

Edited by
Todd E. Jennings

Critical Studies in Education and Culture Series
Edited by Henry A. Giroux

BERGIN & GARVEY
Westport, Connecticut • London

Library of Congress Cataloging-in-Publication Data

Restructuring for integrative education : multiple perspectives,
    multiple contexts / edited by Todd E. Jennings.
        p.   cm. — (Critical studies in education and culture series,
    ISSN 1064–8615)
        Includes bibliographical references and index.
        ISBN 0–89789–496–0 (alk. paper)
        1. Educational change—United States.   2. School management and
    organization—Social aspects—United States.   3. Critical pedagogy—
    United States.   4. Education, Higher—Aims and objectives—United
    States.   5. School supervision—United States.   I. Jennings, Todd
    E., 1960– . II. Series.
    LA210.R468   1997
    370'.973—dc21   96–37123

British Library Cataloguing in Publication Data is available.

Library of Congress Catalog Card Number: 96–37123
ISBN: 0–89789–496–0
ISSN: 1064–8615

First published in 1997

Bergin & Garvey, 88 Post Road West, Westport, CT 06881
An imprint of Greenwood Publishing Group, Inc.

Printed in the United States of America

Copyright Acknowledgment

The editor and publisher gratefully acknowledge permission to quote from the
following:

Chapter 6 first appeared in Chapter 1, "The story of the Savang family."
Adapted by permission of Danling Fu: *My trouble is my English: Asian students
and the American Dream.* (Boynton/Cook Publishers, A subsidiary of Reed
Elsevier Inc., Portsmouth, NH, 1995.)

Contents

Series Foreword

Within the last decade, the debate over the meaning and purpose of education has occupied the center of political and social life in the United States. Dominated largely by an aggressive and ongoing attempt by various sectors of the Right, including "fundamentalist," nationalists, and political conservatives, the debate over educational policy has been organized around a set of values and practices that take as their paradigmatic model the laws and ideology of the marketplace and the imperatives of a newly emerging cultural traditionalism. In the first instance, schooling is being redefined through a corporate ideology that stresses the primacy of choice over community, competition over cooperation, and excellence over equity. At stake here is the imperative to organize public schooling around the related practices of competition, reprivatization, standardization, and individualism.

In the second instance, the New Right has waged a cultural war against schools as part of a wider attempt to contest the emergence of new public cultures and social movements that have begun to demand that schools take seriously the imperatives of living in a multiracial and multicultural democracy. The contours of the cultural offensive are evident in the call by the Right for standardized testing, the rejection of multiculturalism, and the development of curricula around what is euphemistically called a "common culture." In this perspective, the notion of a common culture serves as a referent to denounce any attempt by subordinate groups to challenge the narrow ideological and political parameters by which such a culture both defines and expresses itself. It is not too surprising that the theoretical and political distance between defining schools around a common culture and denouncing cultural difference as the enemy of democratic life is relatively short indeed.

This debate is important not simply because it makes visible the role that schools play as sites of political and cultural contestation, but because it is within this debate that the notion of the United States as an open and democratic society is being questioned and redefined. Moreover, this debate provides a challenge to progressive educators both in and outside of the United States to address a number of conditions central to a postmodern world. First, public schools cannot be seen as either objective or neutral. As institutions actively involved in constructing political subjects and presupposing a vision of the future, they must be dealt with in terms that are simultaneously historical, critical, and transformative. Second, the relationship between knowledge and power in schools places undue emphasis on disciplinary structures and on individual achievement as a primary unit of value. Critical educators need a language that emphasizes how social identities are constructed within unequal relations of power in the schools and how schooling can be organized through interdisciplinary approaches to learning and cultural differences that address the dialectical and multifaceted experiences of everyday life. Third, the existing cultural transformation of American society into a multiracial and multicultural society structured in multiple relations of domination demands that we address how schooling can become sites for cultural democracy rather then channeling colonies reproducing new forms of nativism and racism. Finally, critical educators need a new language that takes seriously the relationship between democracy and the establishment of those teaching and learning conditions that enable forms of self- and social determination in students and teachers. This suggests not only new forms of self-definition for human agency, it also points to redistributing power within the school and between the school and the larger society.

Critical Studies in Education and Culture is intended as both a critique and as a positive response to these concerns and the debates from which they emerge. Each volume is intended to address the meaning of schooling as a form of cultural politics and cultural work as a pedagogical practice that serves to deepen and extend the possibilities of democratic public life. Broadly conceived, some central considerations present themselves as defining concerns of the Series. Within the last decade, a number of new theoretical discourses and vocabularies have emerged that challenge the narrow disciplinary boundaries and theoretical parameters that construct the traditional relationship among knowledge, power, and schooling. The emerging discourses of feminism, post-colonialism, literary studies, cultural studies, and post-modernism have broadened our understanding of how schools work as sites of containment and possibility. No longer content to view schools as objective institutions engaged in the transmission of an unproblematic cultural heritage, the new discourses illuminate how schools function as cultural sites actively engaged in the production of not only knowledge but social identities. *Critical Studies in Education and Culture* will attempt to encourage this type of analysis by emphasizing how schools might be addressed as border institutions or sites of crossing actively involved in exploring, reworking, and translating the ways in which culture is produced, negotiated, and rewritten.

Emphasizing the centrality of politics, culture, and power, *Critical Studies in Education and Culture* will deal with pedagogical issues that contribute in novel ways to our understanding of how critical knowledge, democratic values, and social practices can provide a basis for teachers, students, and other cultural workers to redefine their role as engaged and public intellectuals.

As part of a broader attempt to rewrite and refigure the relationship between education and culture, *Critical Studies in Education and Culture* is interested in work that is interdisciplinary, critical, and addresses the emergent discourses on gender, race, sexual preference, class, ethnicity, and technology. In this respect, the Series is dedicated to opening up new discursive and public spaces for critical interventions into schools and other pedagogical sites. To accomplish this, each volume will attempt to rethink the relationship between language and experience, pedagogy and human agency, and ethics and social responsibility as part of a larger project for engaging and deepening the prospects of democratic schooling in a multiracial and multicultural society. Concerns central to this Series include addressing the political economy and deconstruction of visual, aural, and printed texts, issues of difference and multiculturalism, relationships between language and power, pedagogy as a form of cultural politics, and historical memory and the construction of identity and subjectivity.

Critical Studies in Education and Culture is dedicated to publishing studies that move beyond the boundaries of traditional and existing critical discourses. It is concerned with making public schooling a central expression of democratic culture. In doing so it emphasizes works that combine cultural politics, pedagogical criticism, and social analysis with self-reflective tactics that challenge and transform those configurations of power that characterize the existing system of education and other public cultures.

Henry A. Giroux

Acknowledgments

The editor would like to thank the Center for Integrated Learning and Teaching at California State University, San Bernardino for serving as the book's sponsor. The members of the Center provided insightful assistance during the juried selection of the chapters.

Further thanks are extended to Julius Kaplan in the Office of Graduate Studies at California State University, San Bernardino for grant assistance that was crucial in the final days of manuscript preparation. A debt of gratitude also goes to Terri Jennings and the editors at Bergin and Garvey for their patient guidance and to the series editor Henry A. Giroux for his belief in the project's merit.

Final and deepest thanks go to Larry Moon, who models and draws me into the most powerful and gratifying forms of collaboration imaginable.

Introduction

Todd E. Jennings

Writing on school restructuring abounds. Many of these articles and reports, driven by a sense of exigency to "do something quickly," are organizational and operational in nature. However, as educators respond to political and social changes that call for educational restructuring, we cannot afford to ignore the important and substantive questions rooted in the purposes for restructuring and hence the direction it should take. In short, we cannot ignore the theoretical discussions that articulate and direct the goals and vision for any restructuring effort. Although not a guarantee, establishing a strong theoretical foundation and focus may be the only way to guard against changes that are simply reactionary and unproductive.

This collection, sponsored by the Center for Research in Integrative Learning and Teaching at California State University, San Bernardino, proposes that integrated education be a guiding vision for educational restructuring. Restructuring is defined as any change in the social structures that shape or direct human interaction and learning. The structures cited in the chapters range from tangibles such as organizational structures and disciplinary boundaries to intangible structures such as discourse patterns, language, culture, power relationships, values, and beliefs.

Integrative education is defined as education that promotes learning and teaching in nonfragmented ways that embrace notions of holism, complexity, and interconnection. Integrative education rejects the common emphasis on transmitted knowledge. Rather, it proposes that knowledge and meaning are constructed by the learner through processes of interaction with others, the material, and the social and physical contexts. Integrated education calls to question the traditional gulfs between teacher and learner and rejects the divisions between physiology, cognition, and emotion in the learning process. Furthermore, integrative education embraces the links, rather than the divisions, between the academic disciplines (e.g., arts and sciences) and between various subjective and objective epistemologies and methods of inquiry.

The contributors approach the topic of integrated education from a variety of theoretical perspectives including complexity theory, critical theory, social constructivism, phenomenology, and postmodernism. In addition, a variety of educational contexts are discussed including the university, secondary school, and elementary school levels. To further add to the collection's variety, the chapters include personal narratives, case studies, theoretical pieces, and reports of original research.

Chapter 1: Ivan Kovacs and Helen Shoemaker address the task of restructuring higher education. They propose that the knowledge explosion manifests itself in the university through disciplinary splintering leading to a disintegration of the body of knowledge. However, attempts at integrating subject matter challenge the participants in their interrelated systems of meaning and value, reality, relationships, and social organization. In an integrative restructuring of higher education participants must meet this challenge and become personally engaged in its dialectic. Shoemaker and Kovacs suggest that integration implies a simultaneous and coordinated transformation of subject matter along with a metamorphosis of the participants in their systems of meaning and value, their reality, relationships, and social organization. The authors explore the specific manifestations of these changes and suggest strategies to prepare for and foster them.

Chapter 2: Robbin Crabtree provides a case study in which integrative education is operationalized through a service learning project that encourages students and faculty to make connections between the disciplines of the academy and life beyond the academy. Her chapter, in addition to providing a model of university service learning for integrative education (discussing both strengths and weaknesses), explores some of the competing ideologies that drive service learning and illustrates the potential of service learning projects to integrate faculty members' often disparate goals of teaching, research, and service.

Chapter 3: Recognizing that much of the discussion of restructuring is outcome driven, Susan Drake proposes that the current "dialogue surrounding outcomes still tends to ignore the impact of the hidden curriculum and the unique personality of the teacher who facilitates the delivery of the curriculum." Drake conceptualizes integrated education by first rejecting the factory metaphor for education with its emphasis on skill mastery and product. She also moves beyond constructivism, claiming that it, like the factory model, focuses on product, with skill demonstration simply replacing mastery. As an alternative to these, Drake embraces a *transformative* model, where the goal of education is personal growth and social change. The transformative model concerns itself not only with cognition and rationality but affect and intuition as well. In addition, sociopolitical forces become relevant to learning, teaching, and schooling. Drake proposes that for transformational models to take hold, teachers themselves must recognize that their ways of being, personal identities, and values are enmeshed with the learning-teaching process. She proposes that restructuring for transformation requires a reorientation to the ontologies, both present and future, of both teachers and students.

Chapter 4: In the endeavor to provide better services for children, the field of education has been restructuring and refining its basic mission for the past decade. More recently, school psychology, as a sub-speciality of special education, has begun its own process of reform. Specifically, school psychology has been struggling to redefine the roles of the scientist-practitioner into a model of intervention and prevention. In this chapter, Dudley Wiest and Dennis Kreil work to outline reforms for school psychology by advocating a set of job roles for school psychologists that are holistic in nature. However, there are many impediments to restructuring of such roles. These barriers include such issues as rigid belief systems, lack of a systems approach to conceptualization of children's development, inflexible laws, and lack of time for school psychologists to adequately fulfill any one role.

Chapter 5: Barbara Larrivee outlines the implications of integrative education for classroom management. Approaching this oft-discussed topic from a constructivist perspective, Larrivee proposes a movement away from traditional teacher-directed classroom structures. Constructivist notions of students as active participants in the teaching-learning process necessitate a reconceptualization of what constitutes effective classroom management. As classrooms are restructuring away from teacher control-student compliance patterns of interaction, the new role definitions for teachers and students create new, more interactive, social settings. In such settings work is largely interactive, cooperative, and collaborative. Such classrooms will require more active roles on the part of students as they are called to develop autonomy from teachers and teacher-centered classroom structures. Larrivee outlines the nature of these changes and their implications for management to the end that conceptions of teachers as social and learning mediators are realized.

Chapter 6: In a personal narrative, Danling Fu recounts how her first learning experiences in the United States, portrayed as alienating and humiliating, disconnected her from not only her own literacy and ways of constructing meaning but from the words she was reading and the world she was trying to join. In sharp contrast, Dr. Fu's second learning experience, depicted as liberating and discovering, helped her explore the world through her reading and writing, empowering her as a learner and thinker. She describes a form of integrated learning and teaching where subjective knowledge is trusted as confidently as objective knowing and notions of the learning process are restructured to take the personal lives and worlds of the learner as inseparable.

Chapter 7: The linguistic and cultural needs of diverse students are often neglected in restructuring efforts, despite the evidence suggesting that the high school dropout rate for Mexican immigrants is highest among groups in the United States. Rosalie Giacchino-Baker's year-long study makes a unique contribution because it asked recent Mexican immigrants themselves to explain how they use and acquire English, which is a key to their academic success and social acculturation. As a result Giacchino-Baker provides a list of students' suggestions for restructuring schooling that calls for increased opportunities to use English and the integration of affective and social elements into current conceptualizations of classrooms and schools. Specifically, the findings address such educational structures as student placement, curricula, methodology, educator and student expectations, and the extent to which student languages and cultures are part of the school community.

Chapter 8: The collection's conclusion is offered by Sam Crowell and Renate Caine. They suggest that there is growing evidence that the conceptual nature of change is currently being redefined and requires new questions, processes, and understandings. Crowell and Caine emphasize the merger of our epistemology and our ontology. They suggest that school-based change processes are not driven by what educators know but by what they become. The authors argue that it is only in the process of "becoming" that change takes place. As a result, Crowell and Caine closely relate school discourse and culture to school restructuring for integrated education. Using a case study to illustrate the nature of the process, they offer a critique of common reform efforts and suggest ontology-centered alternatives that foster sustained "re-formation" and "re-culturing" of schools. These ontologically based processes are discussed in light of brain-based learning, complexity theory (which is emerging in our understanding of the New Sciences) and "reconstructive" postmodernism. As a conclusion to the collection, this chapter offers insight into the nature of school change in the twenty-first century.

1

Developmental Dialectic of Students, Faculty, and Higher Education

Ivan D. Kovacs and Helen J. Shoemaker

As we approach the end of this millennium, the call for restructuring has been sounded in more and more domains, including the field of higher education. Yet structural changes seem to have resulted merely in the splintering of disciplines into subdisciplines or the bringing together of disciplines into some multi- or interdisciplinary programs. Lacking, but needed more and more, is a basic transformation that upholds perennial values and responds to historical developments. The focus of this chapter is on the underlying structures that inform this transformation.

The enormous growth and disciplinary splintering of the field of knowledge exposes itself within the university. The boundaries between domains promote both disciplinary parochialisms and imperialisms leading to impotence in understanding and coping with complex world problems. Fragmentation in, and between, research, teaching, and learning, as well as in application, has been intensifying and is now leading to a general disintegration of the functions of higher education. Going beyond disciplines, the constituencies involved in higher education have become increasingly diverse in terms of culture and particular demands. Although the various groups need each other, their differences and needs interfere with successful communication with one another. The ensuing conflicts contribute to the disintegration that threatens or promises to be complete soon unless a dictatorial force takes control. The only hopeful alternative to disintegration or dictatorship is an integrative restructuring of higher education.

Yet to achieve integrated learning and teaching demands a broad-based restructuring so fundamental that even its advocates may be reluctant to recognize and risk it. To advance, we must first step back, gain a wider perspective, and then move forward, pushing ourselves away from the collapsing ground.

Higher education can be seen as *communicative action*: It transmits information, expresses the interlocutor, and defines the relationship of those in the dialogue (Habermas, 1979). Ideally, the integral connection between information transmission, self-expression, and the structure of relationship between the participants in higher education should assure the ongoing development of each of these three components and promote the intellectual and ethical development of the participants.

The developmental goal of premodern liberal arts education was the liberation of its participants. With modernity, the transmission of information came to the forefront. It emphasized the objectivity of truth, delegitimating the self-expression of the speaker and disguising the controlling power relationship within the dialogue (Brand, 1990; Freire, 1972; Habermas, 1979; Pusey, 1987). The emphasis was narrowly placed on knowledge domains, on subject matter rather than on the subject. Now, in postmodernity, the subject has become completely problematic with an emphasis on the questioning of accessibility, integrity, and existence. In the evolution of individualism we have reached an anticlimax: The act of negating the subject has created some critical problems.

Emphasis on information transmission carries with it the assumption that higher education, and especially its restructuring, requires mainly the use of techniques for the assimilation of subject matter on the part of the knower, ignoring the pressures for accommodation by the knower (Piaget, 1966). This is not only a faulty but a destructive assumption. Higher education in its truest sense, especially today, calls for an ongoing transformation of the world of knowledge, its social organization, and the participants themselves (Schon, 1991; Shoemaker, 1991, 1992).

Traditional disciplinary boundaries evolved to be so self-serving and counterproductive that knowledge of the world as a whole shattered and became accessible only in incompatible fragments. In order to overcome compartmentalization, interdisciplinary interaction has been attempted. At the same time, it has also been resisted and/or adjusted to protect territorial autonomies of disciplines or departments. In genuine interdisciplinary interaction, what is known in any separate domain becomes exposed to a questioning of its "truth," including the legitimacy of the methods through which that knowledge was constructed and its constructing community. Through this questioning, basic assumptions and values acceptable within a particular discipline collide with those of others. Interdisciplinarity must attempt to resolve the conflict between incompatible criteria of credibility by reframing the problem, taking the discourse among disciplines to a higher level.

Those who remain isolated in traditional disciplines are often accused of becoming "merely academic," irrelevant but arrogant, wanting but unable to grasp or contribute meaningfully to the solution of contemporary problems. Those who move toward interdisciplinarity risk conflict and criticism, not only with representatives of other disciplines but also with those colleagues who remain loyal to the traditions of their own domain. Academic competencies are assailed and career trajectories as well as interest groups become disturbed. Thus, career identities can become unclear because they do not fit into any traditional categories. This upsets the personal relationships of those affected, including faculty and students. Efforts of social restructuring must take into consideration the changing identities of the participants and provide them with institutional and personal support. Special assistance must be designed for the novice who has managed to keep faith in the infallibility of compartmentalized authorities (Perry, 1970).

The survival of the academic enterprise is troubled not only in its sources of knowledge but also in the sources of legitimation and funding, for example, the controversy over political correctness and the budget battles of state institutions of higher learning. The boundaries between leaders, constituents, supporters, and beneficiaries of higher education become blurred. For instance, the young student of traditional college age is being replaced by working adults whose workplace is often financially supportive of the educational endeavor in the hopes of enhancing productivity. The rise of professional schools is another example. The question surfaces about who needs whom, how the organization and its membership are to be maintained, how its values will be upheld or changed. Restructuring must include the foundations of the institution and involve all its members.

In restructuring, we must recognize that accommodating to all these demands requires of us a change more fundamental and threatening than first apparent. As human beings, we need a certain stability or at least continuity of (1) *meanings and values*, (2) *relationships with others*, and (3) *existence in space and time*. We construct our meaning and value systems, our network of relationships, and our spatiotemporal world, and these constructions are characterized by contingency and a vulnerability that becomes palpable whenever we are challenged in any of the three areas. When challenged in these contingent and vulnerable areas, we become insecure. We may not consciously recognize our insecurity and its roots, but we react nevertheless. Since restructuring higher education according to its contemporary demands challenges the participants in all three areas, this resultant insecurity needs to be understood and successfully addressed. It is critical to realize that these areas— meanings and values, relationships, and existence—are contingent not only in terms of vulnerability but also their interconnections (Kovacs, 1986). Yet here, for the sake of clarity, we want to reconceptualize them separately. (1) Each of us can be seen as an ongoing process of meaning and valuing. This process involves a continual and reciprocal construction and maintenance of our agency and our meaning and value systems. Accommodation to new ways of knowing may challenge our epistemology and ethics. It can undermine our meaning and value systems; indeed, our meaning and valuing. Accommodation means the modification of our habitual ways of making sense of what we become aware of. It can also mean changing the direction we take in our actions. In other words, a discrepancy emerges between the "maps" we have been using and our emerging vision of the "land." Trying to avoid the ensuing chaos, we might hold to prior meanings and commitments and fight their deconstruction or discard them indiscriminately (Fowler, 1981). (2) Each of us can be seen as an ongoing process of relating. Self and other continually and reciprocally constitute each other. This process expresses our connectedness to and separateness from others. It is also an indication of sameness and difference with others. As such, the process is an ongoing defining of our identity. Thrust into new and alien roles, associations, and dialogues, we are challenged in our sense of identity and our established relationships with others. We defend against the threat of intra- and interpersonal disintegration through, among others, fight or flight and/or dependency or counterdependency (Bennis, 1976; Bion, 1961). (3) Each of us can be seen as an ongoing process of existence, a constructing of our reality: a reciprocal creation of our being and our world. When our sense of reality is undermined, our construction and mastery of it is disturbed, threatening our very being in the world. Our security diminishes and we scramble for control (Brickman, 1982).

We must acknowledge how deeply each of these challenges cuts and as a result, how any meaningful restructuring will be fundamentally transformative and must be carefully guided. It demands that we go beyond the integration and assimilation of subject matter and the methodological transformations of knowledge building in teaching, learning, and research. It also requires accommodation, the facilitation of developmental restructuring of the participants. What does this mean in practical terms?

Restructuring must go on concurrently in several areas. When attempted in the past, disciplinary restructuring has occasionally made big advances, yet often it has encountered a great deal of resistance and eventual derailment. With the reorganization and integration of knowledge domains and with a critical transformation of their methodologies, we are confronting not simply disciplinary and ontic issues. They are also epistemological, ontological, value-laden, and thus anxiety provoking and painful (Abercrombie, 1960; Marris, 1975; Perry, 1970). Until this underlying problem is addressed, any transformation will be nonintegrative (Kovacs, 1977; Shoemaker, 1992).

Integrative restructuring must concentrate on issues of interdisciplinary knowledge, faculty and student development, and organizational change in their relationships to each other. Here we must look again at higher education as communicative action that aims at restructuring itself: integrating knowledge, giving self-expression the position it deserves, and making the communicative relationship one that engenders emancipation of all participants.

In our teaching practice developing knowledge in an integrated way is best begun by bringing to awareness the participants' present situation and identifying in it what they experience as problematic. This form of problem-driven inquiry can serve as a context and process. Participants can be especially motivated if they are not handed the problem but instead begin with a heuristic exploration of genuine concerns of their own. Thus, they can more easily see the relevance of the emerging issues to their person. For instance, students may confront and explore the more abstract question of the object-subject split when it emerges in the context of difficulties in interpersonal communication among them and becomes an urgent existential concern. Whereas if they encounter the object-subject split as abstract material to be learned, they experienced it as devoid of relevance and resist it.

To start with the issues rather than with particular disciplines also produces a natural emergence of interdisciplinary interaction. This kind of programming begins with exploring phenomena rather than with handing down the foundations to the uninitiated. Participants will seek foundational work, and the interdisciplinary interaction that ensues can lead to a more thorough understanding of foundational problems. For instance, we may begin with an actual discussion about poverty among representatives of different disciplines. Soon the clashing methodological approaches of the participants will become apparent. Through explicating and discussing the underlying assumptions that inform their various approaches, participants become aware of various ways of seeing their own operations. They explore the implications of how this methodological juxtaposition challenges their own paradigmatic foundations. Only after that can they proceed to bring together their individual contributions in productive and meaningful ways.

Likewise, students who are participant observers of the interdisciplinary dialogue or who are interns situated in problematic field settings will experience similar epistemological concerns. This concern, genuine and unsettling (Abercrombie, 1960; Perry, 1970), needs to be attended and worked through with supportive guidance that will enable the students to then turn more freely to the original problems at hand. In other words, in the context of a situated problem, fundamental theoretical and methodological issues will become problematic for faculty and students alike. Accommodation, a coming to terms with these issues, is a delicate developmental process and provides the necessary foundations for problem solving utilizing a variety of disciplines (Argyris, 1982; Freire, 1972; Kovacs, 1977; Schon, 1991).

Shared reflection brings together not simply expert teacher-disciplinarians and novices but all participants as learners with experience from their own background yet new to the experience of their fellows, be they students or faculty. The juxtaposition and confrontation of diverse views produces an environment that can foster cognitive dissonance, make underlying assumptions problematic, and provoke intra- and interpersonal and intra- and intergroup conflicts. A thorough cognitive restructuring is implied here. In fact, underlying the differentiation of cognitive, conative, and affective functions is the totality of one's being—one's meaning and valuing agency, one's identity in relation with others, and one's reality (i.e., one's very existence in the world)—and it is being confronted. Problems of communication have to be considered in terms of the participants' vulnerability when challenged in each of these areas. Here we are referring to student and faculty development as personal development.

Student and faculty development can best occur when the three structures—agency, identity, and existence—are recognized as vulnerable through the juxtaposition of disparate disciplines that construct reality differently in terms of focus and methodology. Juxtaposing different disciplines eventually undermines conceptions of truth separately owned by representatives of diverse disciplines (Perry, 1970). This dissonance affects students and faculty differently but equally. Students appear to learn faster than faculty. Whereas faculty have investment and commitment in their field and in being authorities themselves, students may distance themselves from the academic subject matter and manipulate it from that distance. Yet the contradiction can challenge the students' worldview to such an extent that it may confront them in all three vulnerable areas. Faculty have developed more effective defenses against change, perhaps because they feel that their careers and professional positions are at risk.

If challenge is all-encompassing, traditional institutions will not effectively be able to facilitate development in their memberships. To support the developmental process properly, the institution must be restructured toward that goal. If their reality is significantly challenged, participants will demand greater control over their trajectories. They will need a supportive environment in which the risks can be worth taking lest they mobilize whatever control they have to abort the developmental process (Marris, 1975; Kegan, 1982).

The creation of a supportive environment implies multilevel institutional restructuring. Traditional institutions of higher education compartmentalize disciplines and separate faculties, having them act autonomously and rather independently from one another. This structure maintains a spirit of competition rather than cooperation among faculty and ensures fragmentation rather than integration of knowledge and of relationships. Such systems support the development of individual career trajectories and the proliferation of separate programs rather than the more difficult task of establishing and renewing integrative and cooperative endeavors.

Many at the university have recognized the importance of integration and have attempted cooperative and collaborative teaching-learning (Tinto, 1987). Integration of subject matter that would require faculty cooperation has been less successful because of both the complexity involved and the risks encountered. For example, faculty can experience threats to habitual (and comfortable) thought patterns as well as professional advancement when working with faculty from other disciplines or organizational units. In these cases, the integrative process can get aborted. Interdisciplinarity can be replaced by multidisciplinarity or pseudo-interdisciplinarity, dominated by a single disciplinary paradigm. True integrative, interdisciplinary higher education can be achieved only by its legitimation at the institutional level and by ongoing support for all participants. We suggest that the following must be established.

Whether coming from the top down or from the bottom up, innovation must be comprehended and valued. To recruit members, the activity must be authorized and accompanied by institutional incentives. More importantly, faculty must be mentored through training in integrative teaching-learning as well as facilitated through supportive and reflective practice as ongoing adjustment is made to this different way of functioning.

Eventually, the participants together will have to develop the environment and structures necessary for their work. To accomplish the task of creating this novel and supportive context, they will need to utilize existing knowledge and well as develop new knowledge. They will need to draw from the appropriate disciplines and especially from their own experience. They will have to create, and at the same time adjust to, ongoing innovation. Such activity turns out to be not only as excellent a motivator as problem driven inquiry but also a form of integrative restructuring of participating, teaching, and learning.

In sum, restructuring in service of integration implies not simply the restructuring of subject matter. Restructuring and integrating the subject matter will challenge the meaning and value systems, relationships and reality structures of the participants individually and as a social organization. Participant restructuring demands a social setting designed to support this activity. Realization of this design means a restructuring of the existing institution. The participants themselves, with the help of the subject matter, create a dialectical, simultaneous process of restructuring of setting, self, and subject matter. All these factors must be tackled simultaneously and in concert. Attempts at solutions that take only partial account of the complexity involved in integrative teaching-learning will only achieve half solutions that may end up in failure, discrediting and jeopardizing the whole integrative enterprise.

REFERENCES

Abercrombie, M. L. Johnson. (1960). *The Anatomy of Judgment*. London: Hutchinson & Co.

Argyris, C. (1982). *Reasoning, Learning, and Action: Individual and Organizational*. San Francisco: Jossey-Bass, 1982.

Bennis, W. (1976). *Analysis of Groups*. (Edited by G. S. Gibbard, J. J. Hartman, & R. D. Mann). San Francisco: Jossey-Bass.

Bion, W. R. (1961). *Experience in Groups*. London: Tavistock Publications.

Brand, A. (1990). *The Force of Reason: An Introduction to Habermas' "Theory of Communicative Action."* Sydney: Allen & Unwin.

Brickman, P. (1982, April). Models of Helping and Coping. *American Psychologist, 37*(4), 368–384.

Fowler, J. (1981). *Stages of Faith: The Psychology of Human Development and the Quest for Meaning*. New York: Harper & Row.

Freire, P. (1972). *The Pedagogy of the Oppressed*. Harmondsworth, England: Penguin Books.

Habermas, J. (1979). *Communication and the Evolution of Society*. (Translated and introduced by T. McCarthy), Boston: Beacon Press.

Kegan, R. (1982). *The Evolving Self*. Cambridge: Harvard University Press.

Kovacs, I. D. (1986). *An Ontological Basis of Human Development*. Paper presented at the Sixth International Human Science Research Conference, Berkeley, CA: May, 1986.

Kovacs, I. D. (1977). *Development of Cognitive, Coping and Relational Abilities Through the Study of Participation in the University*. Paper presented at the Third International Conference on Improving University Teaching, England.

Marris, P. (1975). *Loss and Change*. New York: Anchor Books.

Perry, W. G. (1970). *Forms of Intellectual and Ethical Development in the College Years*. New York: Holt, Rinehart & Winston.

Piaget, J. (1966). *Psychology of Intelligence*. Totowa, NJ: Adams.

Pusey, M. (1987). *Jürgen Habermas*. London: Tavistock Publications.

Schon, D. (1991). *The Reflective Turn*. New York: Teachers College Press.

Shoemaker, H. J. (1991). Self construction in a small group setting: Journal narratives. *Small Group Research. 22* (3) (August), 339–354.

Shoemaker, H. J. (1992). *A Psychological-Phenomenological Study of African-American Women's Decisions to Enter Higher Education at Midlife*. University Dissertation Microfilms, Ann Arbor, Michigan.

Tinto, V. (1987). *Leaving College: Rethinking the Causes and Cures of Student Attrition*. London: University of Chicago Press.

2

Service Learning and the Liberal Arts: Restructuring for Integrated Education

Robbin D. Crabtree

> The literacy required to live in a civil society, the competence to participate in democratic communities, the ability to think critically and act deliberatively in a pluralistic world, the empathy that permits us to hear and thus accommodate others, all involve skills that must be acquired. Excellence is the product of teaching and is liberty's measure. (p. 4)
>
> —Benjamin R. Barber
> *An Aristocracy of Everyone: The Politics of Education and the Future of America*

INTRODUCTION

After an intriguing discussion of the history of American thought, diversity, and democracy around the centerpiece of education, Ben Barber (1992) recasts the debate over the current "crisis" in American education. He argues that students must learn the meaning and practice of liberty as the most fundamental component of education. His solution to the crisis: a program of community service to "inspire a renewed interest in civic education and citizenship" (p. 245).

The service component of education "promotes an understanding of how self and community, private interest and public good, are necessarily linked" (p. 249). This framework is compatible with the notion of integrative learning and teaching. In a true liberal arts tradition, which Barber argues is endangered even at traditional liberal arts colleges, students (and faculty) are encouraged to make connections between the various disciplines in the academy, and further connections to life outside the academy.

Barber's compelling book set the stage for a few days of workshops, presentations, and discussions about service learning at DePauw University during the summer of 1993. Faculty, administrators, community service staff, students, and Barber himself participated. DePauw already has an impressive service learning component and even received a "thousand points of light" award in 1991. Based on my experience with a service learning project sponsored by DePauw, and on reflections from Barber's book and the discussions of it, this chapter examines the strengths and weaknesses of a particular service learning program: DePauw University's Winter Term in Mission (WTIM). The discussion has a number of objectives: (1) to describe the service learning project that took place in El Salvador in 1993; (2) to discuss the strengths and weaknesses of the project with reference to Barber's vision of education for liberty and suggestions for restructuring the WTIM program; (3) to raise some ongoing concerns about competing ideologies of service; and (4) to illustrate the potential of service learning projects to integrate faculty members' often disparate goals of teaching, research, and service. Finally, changes that have actually taken place since the first writing of this chapter will be reported. DePauw's experience provides an excellent case study in restructuring for integrative education and can be instructive to other programs and universities.

ALTERNATIVE DEVELOPMENT IN EL SALVADOR AND WTIM

In 1991, after twelve years of war and a year of ceasefire and peace negotiations, the Salvadoran people had every reason to be hopeful for the first time in over a decade. Even though the peace accords had been signed, however, tension still characterized the relations between people and government, military personnel, and guerrilla forces in El Salvador. While negotiations to rebuild a nation were taking place at many levels, the Salvadoran peasants were continuing to repopulate the villages they had fled during the conflict, and they had begun to rebuild their homes and their lives.

In another world both figuratively and literally is Greencastle, Indiana. A small rural town of about 7,000 people in west-central Indiana, Greencastle is home to DePauw University, a liberal arts institution with approximately 2,100 students, most of whom are upper middle class and white. What could Greencastle, Indiana, possibly have in common with Consolación, El Salvador? As part of a program sponsored by Companion Community Development Alternatives (Co-Co, a small nongovernmental organization) and DePauw University's WTIM program, the Common Council of Greencastle had formally declared a companion relationship with the small village of Consolación in the Cuscatlán province of El Salvador's Guazapa Valley. As part of this companionship, a team of thirty students and fifteen or so professionals (doctors, nurses, dentists, engineers, and college professors) spent a month in this small community in El Salvador's ex-conflictive zone rebuilding a school and offering basic health care.

With the signing of the peace accords and the initiation of the Plan for National Reconstruction in El Salvador, this was the critical moment to address the social and economic injustices that gave rise to the war; it was also the first realistic opportunity to invest in long-term reconstruction and sustainable community develop-ment projects. Co-Co envisions "a global community founded on just relationships between nations and people and rooted in the democratic use of resources for sustainable socioeconomic devel-opment." Co-Co promotes the organization of individuals, groups, and institutions in the United States around the need for sustain-able development in the Salvadoran communities most affected by the war. It facilitates the sharing of technical, material, financial, and human resources between Salvadoran and U.S. communities as an alternative to traditional north-south relations that have been perpetuated by governments and large aid organizations.

Co-Co refers to its alternative development model as a "people's policy" for cooperative development. The emphasis on fostering relationships between communities and individuals across the two cultures creates a context for education about global economic structures, democratic methods for social change, and participatory development. The organization encourages North Americans to contemplate what they can learn from Salvadorans in terms of community, faith, and self-determination, rather than conceptualizing the exchange as unidirectional from North to South. Co-Co believes that the Salvadorans can teach North Americans a great deal about democracy, community, and civil service. The Salvadoran context was ideal for integrated education in liberty. That is, the historical and theoretical preparation provided intellectual stimulation; the cross-cultural experience engaged students' emotions; the political nature of the context piqued contemplation of citizenship and social responsibility; the work project challenged students' physical endurance; and the project organization annihilated the traditional power relationships between students and teachers, as well as between North Americans and Salvadorans.

Winter Term in Mission began about sixteen years ago in DePauw University's Chaplain's Office as an opportunity for students to spend the January term doing a service education project. Formerly a Methodist-affiliated institution, DePauw maintains some connection to its church-affiliated history. Sponsored by the Campus Ministries Center, DePauw students have done work in Peru, Mexico, Guatemala, the Dominican Republic, Nicaragua, and now El Salvador, in addition to dozens of other domestic and foreign locations. Teams are normally composed of thirty to forty people (fewer for domestic sites) and divided into three work teams: medical, public health, and construction. In addition, two faculty advisors and a chaplain accompany the team.

Each medical team includes a health care unit composed of two doctors, two dentists, two nurses, a pharmacist, and six to eight DePauw University premedical, predental, and nursing students. Medical teams have been set up in local clinics, improvised on-site clinics, and/or organized traveling medical units going from village to village by truck or canoe or on foot.

The public health unit incorporates one professional public health educator and four DePauw students who have taken a semester-long course in public health education and who have translating ability in the local language, which is usually Spanish. This unit teaches elementary public health, sanitation techniques, basic nutrition, first aid, and family planning. Often these teams are used to train local village leaders to serve as public health educators after the team has left the site.

The construction team consists of an engineer and at least fifteen students who work with local volunteers to build a school, church, community center, clinic, or similar construction. Generally, the exact project is determined by the cosponsoring organization (which could be a North American church or another type of humanitarian organization), with some degree of collaboration with village leaders.

The structure of the team leadership uses a student-centered model. Student leaders are chosen for the positions of project officer, chief of construction, chief of medical and public health, chief of operations (arranges finances, accommodation, etc.), cultural affairs officer, and worship officer. A chaplain, who may or may not be from DePauw, works with the worship officer to create guided reflection opportunities for the team members. The faculty advisors help develop an educational program for the students; work with the construction, public health or medical teams alone or in combination; support the student executive body; and serve as the ultimate authority. The student executive committee outlined above begins planning for the project about six months before the team departs campus, organizing construction and medical supplies, gathering educational materials, and preparing the other team members (orientation, shots, packing, etc.).

DePauw's WTIM program incorporates much of Barber's framework for service learning projects. Barber himself actually relies heavily on Rutgers' community service program as a model (see pp. 253–261). DePauw's program involves experiential learning, taking students into the "real world" to observe and to act. Like the Rutgers program, WTIM uses a team approach in which students experience life in a particular community while also learning to build and practice community. They work in task-oriented groups in planning and executing the project. Like the Rutgers program, WTIM is completely voluntary. The assumption of the Rutgers program is that community service is the most powerful form of experiential learning, as opposed to internships, lab assignments, and the like. Within a disciplined pedagogical setting, community service teaches citizenship and social responsibility (Barber, 1992).

Winter Term in Mission also manifests several features of integrative learning and teaching. It is inherently multidisciplinary because the students and faculty come from all possible parts of the academy. Students who may never see each other in the classroom because of disparate major programs share perspectives. Faculty are able to interact with students from different disciplines while also broadening their own interests. Because students are responsible for much of the project organization, WTIM erases the traditional distinctions between the roles of professor and student, who instead become collaborators in a team structure. Further, integrative education rejects the conventional educational divisions between physiology, cognition, and emotion. In this regard, WTIM is most successful. Participants engage in hard physical labor and are exposed to new living conditions that challenge the body. Formal learning such as reading, critical thinking, discussion, and writing is built into the project. Both the context and the experience provide for a heightening of emotional awareness that is then connected to the learning process. This is encouraged through journal writing, formal and informal group discussion, and reflection sessions.

TOWARD RESTRUCTURING THE WTIM MODEL

Although the WTIM model has produced several successful projects and enriching learning experiences for students, it has not been without its faults. The overview of WTIM given in the preceding section is an idealistic one; few projects have managed to produce a completely integrated educational experience for students or faculty. In restructuring the program to maximize its pedagogical and ethical effectiveness, several issues need to be considered. Among these concerns, the most noteworthy are the religious and paternalistic overtones of the mission model of development, the implications for host communities of the student-driven and student-centered model of the program, and the lack of a strong educational component as foundation for the students before and during the trip.

Many of the most appropriate members of the faculty—namely, professors of sociology, anthropology, and development economics—have declined participation in WTIM primarily because of its religious overtones. Clearly, the mission model is only one development model, yet one that has been the subject of much criticism throughout the ages. Perhaps the most blatant example of the problem inherent in the mission model comes from Honduras, where a Presbyterian Church sponsored the building of a church in a Catholic community. The project divided the community, and the students were subject to a great deal of hostility during their workstay. Related to this is the potential problem of the students becoming unwitting and perhaps free labor for special interests within communities—and in this case, within developing nations.

Further, the worship component of the program tended to force a Christian perspective on students as they attempt to understand and process their experience. Throughout the three and one-half weeks of work students engaged in activities to help them reflect on their experiences. Some of these activities were church-based rituals or close to them. This approach was not always welcome or appropriate. Some students reported in journals and exit interviews that they found the rituals alienating, contrived, and inappropriate to their own belief systems. Also problematic within this Christian perspective is a charity model of development which manifests itself in a paternalistic attitude of unidirectional giving. This has functioned to perpetuate traditional North-South relations, additionally obscuring the imperialism of missionary work it also blinds the students to what the rural poor in the so-called third world might teach them. In this regard, Barber notes:

Simply to enlist volunteers to serve "others less fortunate" or "those at risk" (we are *all* at risk!), or to conscript young people for some form of national service in the name of improving their moral character or forcing them to "repay the debt they owe their country" (the language of market contracts applied to politics and the public good) will do little to reconstruct citizenship or shore up democracy and do nothing at all to improve the caliber of our educational community. (p. 254, emphasis in original)

Barber persuasively argues that one of the key motivations for doing community service rises from a longing for community, which the market language subverts or ignores. The El Salvador project discussed here deliberately attempted to redress these concerns.

Another area of concern with the WTIM program has been its reliance on the student governance model. Students expect to be the primary decision-makers at the various worksites. Part of this is an outgrowth of the model; however, much of it seems to be a function of the egocentrism and ethnocentrism of the students themselves. Confronting ethnocentrism is a primary goal of the WTIM program. Therefore, the process of learning to collaborate with local people is important. However, the emphasis on individualism, in the forms of survival (hard work and substandard living conditions) and leadership (student-centered decision making) can reinforce the egocentrism of the project. It is a positive manifestation of integrated education to have students, as opposed to faculty and administrators, in power and decision-making roles. However, when this leadership structure is transferred to the village context, villagers must necessarily share equally with students in decision-making and leadership functions. In this situation, the goals of integrated education (i.e., students in power) and those of participatory development (i.e., *campesinos* in power) compete.

A related concern posits that the project itself exploits rural populations and communities for the learning experience of elite North American college students. Sure, the students bring materials, labor, and money to the local economy, but the project can be a disruption of local rhythms, a drain of energy and labor away from community-driven projects, and a perpetuation of the "great white hope" model of development. Without a sound development policy or model, without an emphasis on education about the culture and sociopolitical history of the particular nation and community to be helped, and without serious reflection about development and service, the program is student-centered. In short, the students are potentially the sole beneficiaries of the project.

The above concerns are magnified by what students say about WTIM, for the oral history passed on student participants is a powerful obstacle to restructuring. The stories students share about past WTIM trips center around resumé-building credentialing ("I was the project officer . . . "), liberal consumption of alcohol, suntanning opportunities, romantic and sexual liaisons, and bargain shopping. This is not to say the student participants don't value the cross-cultural, educational, and physical challenges presented them by WTIM. However, the challenges are noted more in the academic journals and in conversations with faculty rather than in what the student participants say on the student circuit. Among students, WTIM may be perceived as "party" program.

Despite these potential—and substantial—pitfalls, however, the WTIM program may be reworked to create both sound development work and positive learning experiences. The key, it seems, is to combine increased education about the target culture and society—and its relationship to the dominant U.S. culture—with an alternative development model, perhaps a community-centered model, and to emphasize intercultural communication and exchange. The WTIM project in Consolación, Cuscatlán, El Salvador, during January 1993 employed such a combination of features with remarkable results.[1]

OVERCOMING SHORTCOMINGS: THE EL SALVADOR PROJECT

In the ongoing process of evaluating and restructuring the WTIM program, discussion frequently returns to the El Salvador project as a case in point. Perhaps the most important feature of the El Salvador project was that the project proposal originated in the community itself; DePauw's WTIM program coordinators were approached by Co-Co on behalf of Consolación. The community *directiva* in Consolación worked with Co-Co representatives to plan and implement the project. This led to a heightened sense of project ownership by community members. Although past WTIM projects had originated with cosponsoring organizations, most agencies have not been as well integrated into the local communities or as committed to local grassroots efforts as Co-Co.

The development model used in El Salvador also placed an emphasis on collaborative and cooperative decision making and work. This meant that local health promoters integrated the De-Pauw medical and public health teams into their own ongoing plan for health care and education in the zone. The college students and doctors were able to learn just how well trained, well organized and self-determined the rural health workers had become and about the context of war in which they had developed their skills.

Similarly, people from Consolación and Salvadoran engineers and welders worked with the student construction team to design and build the school. Each decision making meeting and each work-site were integrated with North Americans and Salvadorans (both men and women). Further, to replace some of the labor force the community lost by working on the school, students rotated into the community to work in the fields, in the kitchen, and so on. Thus, a true exchange was encouraged in an attempt to meet the needs of the community, the requirements of the project itself, and the learning objectives of the students and faculty.

Generally, the Salvadorans had the most power in final decisions, and the cultural norms of Consolación prevailed. We worked in accordance with local culture (e.g., time orientation) and adapted to the changing needs and circumstances that we confronted. Decisions were not always made in the most efficient manner in North American terms, but they were generally the most locally appropriate and grew from local custom and self-determination. The students were frustrated with this in the beginning but came to respect the Salvadoran customs and self-determination. This lead to decentering the students from leadership and decisionmaking. The unique context—postwar El Salvador—humbled the students as they learned about the history of this community and the root causes of underdevelopment in the zone. Not coincidentally, understanding the conditions in El Salvador inevitably led the analysis back to the role of the United States and to a contemplation of the students' responsibilities as U.S. citizens.[2] As an integrated learning experience, the project emphasized personal growth and civic action in an experiential learning process.

The academic or intellectual component of integrated education manifest on the El Salvador trip was critical to the success of the project (success was measured at the community-project level as well as in individual-collective student learning). Students completed a number of readings organized by the cultural affairs officer and the faculty advisors during the fall semester. Faculty advisors facilitated guided journal entries as responses to the readings. The entire team met on several occasions to discuss the land tenure system, the nature of the armed conflict, the role of the United States in El Salvador's political history, the ideological nature of development and the features of the alternative development model, cultural norms in El Salvador, and so on. Contrary to the "fun in the sun" or "grand tour" models many students had come to expect from WTIM trips, this project was an intellectual and consciousness-raising experience first and foremost. Further, formal education did not end when the plane landed in San Salvador. Certainly informal and experiential learning are integral to all WTIM projects. The process of adapting to another culture and the nature of the work itself make this inevitable. But once in El Salvador, the formal education continued, as well. More guided journal entries and presentations from exmilitary officers, ex–Farabundo Marti Front for National Liberation (FMLN) guerrillas, war-wounded from both sides, women who were ex-combatants, community members, former refugees, ecology workers, journalists, and United States Agency for International Development officials rounded out the learning agenda. Students heard the stories of people from various perspectives firsthand. This allowed them to integrate what they already knew including U.S. media accounts and their parents' appraisals, with what they heard from actual participants and what they experienced for themselves in the community. Having access to so many different perspectives allowed the student participants to build their own conclusions and to develop a unique perspective grounded in in-depth *study* as well as firsthand *experience*. Not surprisingly, hearing the people's stories inevitably engaged students' emotions in the learning process, integrating subjective and objective ways of knowing. The tragedy and triumph, personal loss and political devastation experienced by the Salvadorans made for profound reminiscences. Although this was a politically radicalizing experience for some, faculty advisors and program organizers allowed and encouraged students to be comfortable with their own belief systems.

Additionally, the focus on learning and practicing effective intercultural communication created a healthy environment for the emotional and psychological transformation that cross-cultural experiences can foster (e.g., see Adler, 1975; Brislin, 1981; Church, 1982; Furnham & Bochner, 1986; Martin, 1989). Students were encouraged to withhold interpretation and evaluation of Salvadoran customs and instead to observe, describe, and value the differences they noted. Learning about context, history, and culture helped students come to appreciate rather than pity, the Salvadoran way of life, even that practiced by the very poor people of rural Cuscatlán. Gaining a background in intercultural communication theory and practicing effective intercultural skills led to the development of mutual respect among students and community members. Because the students were collaborators with the people of Consolación—and not merely guests doing service in this community—the cross-cultural exchange took place within an environment of shared power and purpose.[3] As with much of the project design, the intercultural communication component fits nicely with the goals of integrated learning. Students were taught some of the theory of intercultural communication as well as given an opportunity to practice and reflect on their knowledge and skills. This unites theory and practice. Further, intercultural experiences facilitate personal growth (Adler, 1975). The cross-cultural experience, when framed by academics, thus brings the entire person into the learning process—cognition, action, and emotion.

Because Barber's (1992) notion of integrated education has the ultimate goal of producing productive citizens, it is worthwhile to point out these connections with the El Salvador project. Although doing development work can be seen generally as social action, the students were given an opportunity to exercise their rights and responsibilities as U.S. citizens. The team sponsored a unique visit to the U.S. Embassy and the offices of USAID that incorporated three members of the Consolación *directiva* and two other Salvadoran development workers. This visit allowed the Salvadorans to use their own voices to ask USAID officers about their development plans in the previously conflictive zone and in repopulated communities like Consolación. As one Salvadoran *compañero* put it, "This was the first time that 'little hats' were allowed in the palace." The students were able to witness this exchange and to ask about U.S. development policy in Central America and El Salvador; they were thus able to demonstrate their involvement with U.S. government activities and to hold their government agencies accountable. Their study and experiences had prepared them well for this encounter, which was an eye-opening experience for the students, whose firsthand observations in the community made them witnesses to past (failed) development policy and long-term neglect. The encounter was also empowering for the Salvadorans, who became increasingly aware that not all North Americans were their enemies. The WTIM project in El Salvador enacted the people-to-people diplomacy that Co-Co has envisioned.

EMPOWERMENT, COMMUNITY, AND CROSS-CULTURAL SERVICE LEARNING

Barber (1992) argues that empowerment is a "necessary condition of the free community" (p. 231). Yet, he continues, as the university has evolved, both faculty and students have been increasingly disempowered. The market-framed conception of service as a "repayment" undermines a sense of empowerment that might be derived from service learning. Further, the focus of service learning should be on the community—the learning community as well as the community-context for service. Empowerment and community are critical components of integrated education; they were the two central themes by design and outcome of the El Salvador WTIM project.

The empowerment that seemed to grow from the project in Consolación has manifested itself in a number of ways. Many of the student participants have for the first time become aware of U.S. foreign policy and international development issues. Based on the experience in the U.S. embassy, several students have used their own political voices by writing to their representatives in Congress about development policy in El Salvador and by remaining active in solidarity work. In the formal and informal presentations they have relayed their experiences to friends, coworkers, schools, church congregations, and civic organizations. Key in these presentations has been the video documentary produced during the project—a documentary that won Best Student Documentary and Best Documentary from the Indiana Film Society. The experience of the student participants—and the students' need to communicate it—has given them a voice and a sense of themselves as citizens. This integrated education experience engaged their bodies, minds, and emotions in learning and action and enabled them to see education as an ongoing process unframed by term calendars and class schedules.

Lest we forget, service learning projects should, *by design*, empower the community in addition to empowering the students (Barber, 1992). The Salvadorans experienced empowerment through the participatory model of development as well as through the cross-cultural component. Participatory development involves project beneficiaries in some or all facets of development efforts (e.g., see Berrigan, 1981; Crabtree, 1993; Hornik, 1988; Nair &

White, 1987; Tandon, 1981). This was certainly the case in Conso-lación. The community *directiva* generally had the final say in what, when, and how the construction project proceeded. The health promoters of the zone had the same power. The visit to USAID brought the community members pride and esteem—and sub-sequently a USAID-funded housing project. The presence of North Americans in the zone brought needed attention to the area in the form of observers from the Office of National Reconstruction and USAID. Apparently, the "people's policy" of cooperative develop-ment could have an influence at the national policy level and at the international policy level as well.

The project brought many *campesinos* in close contact with North Americans for the first time. For DePauw students and *campesinos* alike, it was empowering to recognize similarities between people of diverse backgrounds and experiences. Sharing laughter, stories, and hard work with North Americans stood in sharp contrast to the twelve years of war funded by *"los yanquis."* In fact, telling their stories to their North American visitors was very therapeutic for many of those who had undergone years of trauma and violence and who were struggling to reclaim their land and their lives.

ONGOING CONCERNS AND THE PROCESS OF RESTRUCTURING

The WTIM project in El Salvador continues to influence discus-sions of integrated and service learning at DePauw. First, the definition of "community" in relation to service is wrought with dilemmas. The discussions at DePauw in summer 1993 led to the prevailing wisdom that we must not define community as "out there." The university is a community and might be the best place to start service learning. Racial tensions, date rape, eating disor-ders, and more, are all problems that confront college campuses and impinge upon the development of an empowering learning community. The community is not "the other," we, too, are "the community."

In whatever community we serve, we must be aware of the impact we might have, both positive and negative. With the El Salvador project, Consolación gained the attention of the Sal-vadoran National Committee for Reconstruction as well as USAID.

A housing project sponsored by USAID has now been completed in the area. Our presence there served as the single most influential factor in getting much-needed housing for that community. However, our presence did not necessarily cause USAID or the Salvadoran government to rethink their overall development policies and priorities. In fact, this one housing project can now be held up as an example of selective USAID and government responsiveness while other needy communities go unserved. Service learning projects can easily be co-opted by special interests, not to mention the long-term impacts such projects can have in the community. Raising community expectations unrealistically, participating in the short-term solution of what are really long-term and very complex problems, and contaminating naturally occurring events and customs are all implications we must consider. Indeed, the very idea that service, rather than broad economic and social transformation, can provide solutions to social problems must be examined.

The marketing of service learning programs is also a significant concern. As service learning increasingly comes into "vogue," university administrations and admissions departments will not fail to turn it into a marketing strategy, particularly at private universities like DePauw. This practice has the potential of trivializing service learning components, minimizing the empowerment, community, and social responsibility approach in favor of a more charitable and vocational tack that is easier to explain concisely in promotional literature, and undermining the credibility of the program itself (faculty bristle in response to university marketing campaigns and may tend to reject the program rather than admonish the marketing tactics). Further, university administrations have the tendency to market ideas before they have explored them fully or even instituted them. The university community must be given ample time to explore the philosophies, goals, and consequences of service learning programs before such programs are marketed to potential "consumers." Then the marketing should be held to the same standards as the program itself.

Finally, the academic integrity of service learning must be upheld. Experiential learning as a concept reeks of vocationalism, still abhorred at many liberal arts institutions, but it need not be professionalized. Service learning can be grounded in the theoretical concepts of various fields of study and should include in-depth study of historical, social, political, and cultural factors related to the service and the service community. This practice will provide the essential links between the epistemological arena and civic action and social responsibility. It will also garner the support of the best faculty and can inspire a reinvigoration of traditional curricula. The implications for developing integrated teaching and learning are obvious. Service learning can and should be interdisciplinary, restructure power relationships between students and teachers, engage many epistemologies (knowing through study, action, and reflection), and ultimately alter the rigid conceptualization of ivory tower education itself. As manifest in El Salvador during the winter of 1992, these values and practices spread to the *campesinos* in Consolación. Students learned to value the knowledge of those without formal education, and peasants came to teach what they have lived and learned. Such an experience suggests that a true critical pedagogy (Freire, 1970), consistent with the goals of integrated learning and teaching, can be achieved.

Since January 1993 DePauw University has put significant energy into restructuring the WTIM program. Some of the changes came directly from reflections on the success of the El Salvador project. Others were more closely aligned with Barber's notion of "civic education," which became the centerpiece of institutional reflection for a period of time in 1993–94. The following changes reflect and illustrate a process of restructuring for integrated education across several key areas: academic disciplines, college structures, power relationships, types of learning, knowledge-epistemologies valued, and outcomes assessment. Some of these reflect more restructuring than others, although the WTIM program at DePauw was already well grounded in integrated education principles.

College Structures

The most significant restructuring that has taken place at De-Pauw over the 1993–95 period has been the institution of a formal integrated service learning program. DePauw's WTIM program has been moved from the Chaplain's Office to the Office of Volunteer Service Programs (the move is both physical and administrative). The program is now being called Winter Term in Service (WTIS). A new position was created in Academic Affairs at the associate dean level for service learning, and another at the Program Administrator level specifically for the WTIS program. Not insignificant is that the former administrative assistant to the chaplain was promoted to the new position as Associate Director of WTIS. She read with interest the analysis and writing I have done on WTIM and was instrumental in bringing these ideas to the program oversight committee to initiate many of the changes. This process itself represents an integrative approach to decision making where faculty, administrators, and students are able to cooperate. For me, it has become a true unification of teaching, research, university service, and civic action.

Disciplines

Integrated education is interdisciplinary and encourages students and faculty to make links between various areas of study. The WTIM program, now the WTIS, has always united students and teachers across academic majors and disciplines. What seems to be occurring with the restructuring, however, is that more faculty want to be involved. Although certain academic specialties seem more closely aligned with the nature of these service projects (e.g., anthropology, development economics, intercultural communication, and foreign languages), the program will surely benefit and grow from wider participation. This may also be seen in the number of students who seek involvement; the student waiting list went from twenty-six to eighty-six in the year after WTIS implementation.[4]

Power Relationships

WTIS continues to be student directed with the same leadership structure as before. The degree to which individual projects incorporate participatory development models—a more profound level of power restructuring—remains to be evaluated project by project. The feasibility of having this model of development be a prerequisite for project design should be examined. Through the ongoing exchange of information and continued dialogues among faculty, students, and administrators, such an examination will be possible. After all, restructuring power relationships within the learning context will not achieve much if the power relationships in the target communities remain the same. The Chaplain's Advisory Committee report delineated a new expected outcome of the WTIS program: Students will develop a greater awareness of the systemic inequalities in the world, including their causes and consequences.

Types of Learning

A variety of learning styles and strategies are already well entrenched in the program. For faculty, this has always meant providing academic grounding for the trip in addition to playing a role as facilitator and team member. Students complete traditional academic style work (reading, writing, and examination) in addition to doing difficult physical labor, guided and independent reflection, consciousness-raising discussion, and so forth. However, one change has been an emphasis on civic and social responsibility rather than on moral or religious duty. Whereas the mission program entailed a focus on religious reflection and charity, the service learning program focuses on rights and responsibilities and attempts to bring the experience back to campus life through continued study and action. Time and future research will indicate the extent to which these goals are met, exactly how they are manifest, and their implications to integrated learning and teaching theory.

Knowledge-Epistemologies Valued

Multiple epistemologies have already been valued and nurtured by the program. For example, students have always been encouraged to explore their emotions about living in another culture, about pushing their physical abilities in hard labor, about building a team and community among themselves. Having reflected upon the moral and ethical dimensions of their project, and they have been encouraged to make connections between the theoretical and the practical. Currently, a greater emphasis is being placed on the civic manifestation of the experiential learning project. An increased emphasis on garnering and valuing the experience and knowledge of their hosts was in evidence on the El Salvador trip and is encouraged for the future. The Chaplain's Advisory Committee report recommended that the cultural affairs officer of each trip work more closely with the faculty advisors to reinforce the importance of learning on these trips.

Outcomes Assessment

A relatively new buzzword for universities, outcomes assessment has become the focus of attention at the college and department levels of universities. As faculty and administrators seek to assess their programs, service learning must be incorporated into the institutional assessment process. This should take place in assessing student performance, faculty performance, and institutional accreditation. The implications of this seem most far-reaching for faculty who are evaluated for tenure and promotion on the basis of teaching, research, and service. Service has heretofore been the least concern in assessing faculty performance. However, if we begin to make the links between teaching, research, and service—and if we believe that integrated education is truly the most effective—then we must also credit faculty with their efforts in this regard. Faculty who participate in service learning projects must be rewarded. Faculty who incorporate service and other integrated education elements into their regular classroom activities must be valued and encouraged. So often young, untenured scholars are not encouraged to be innovative and can be admonished for too much energy applied toward teaching, especially at so-called research institutions, and receive little credit at all for service. If outcomes assessment procedures are to catch up with this cutting edge approach to integrated education, we will also need to examine more closely what we mean by service and be prepared to evaluate it not merely on its presence or absence but on its qualitative features as well.

NOTES FOR FACULTY: INTEGRATING TEACHING, RESEARCH, AND SERVICE

It would be useful to examine how service learning projects can produce opportunities for research. The assumption here is that faculty must, and inevitably will, contemplate the benefits to themselves as the idea of incorporating service learning into the curriculum spreads from campus to campus. It is not only wise for scholars to combine research, teaching, and service, but within a framework of integrated teaching and learning, it creates a more ethical pedagogy—and more ethical, relevant scholarship as well. The service learning project offers an opportunity to unite teaching, research, and action; to participate in the process whereby the knowledge we generate has a real impact on our society—and potentially on the world.[5]

Additionally, service learning provides the opportunity to examine the pedagogical implications of service on learning. There are, in effect, many avenues to explore our research interests in service learning contexts, which are also teaching-learning environments and service or action components of our responsibilities as faculty. Thus, service learning provides an opportunity to become more socially responsible as teachers and scholars.

Without education that treats women and men as whole, as beings who belong to communities of knowledge, . . . without schools that take responsibility for what goes on beyond as well as in the classroom, and work to remove the walls that separate the two worlds, students [and faculty] will continue to bracket off all that they learn from life and keep their lives at arm's length from what they learn. (Barber, 1992, p. 260)

NOTES

1. It should be noted that two of the coordinators of the Indianapolis office of Co-Co were DePauw graduates with WTIM experience. This meant that the cosponsoring organization knew the features of the WTIM program, including its shortcomings. Through collaboration among the faculty advisors, the student executive committee, and Co-Co, we were able to address and correct many of these shortcomings in advance.

2. Whether this model would work in most contexts remains a question. The revolutionary context and the historic moment in El Salvador were critical factors in the design and success of the project. Further, it is arguable that a level of social organization similar to that achieved by rural communities in El Salvador and the prevalence of substantial grassroots development efforts are prerequisites for successful participatory, self-sustaining development projects.

3. The faculty advisors had a background in international and development communication and interpersonal and intercultural communication respectively, as well as experience in Central American solidarity work; they had also lived in Central American cultures. As well, they had functional to fluent ability in Spanish.

4. This rise in interest came despite the first student death in WTIM's history. During January 1995 on site at a project in Bolivia, an unexpected storm caught the team in an unprotected area. When lightning struck the site, one DePauw student and one local baby were killed. Others were wounded. The project was discontinued, and the team returned to the United States.

5. Suggestions for ways of studying the relationships among participatory development, intercultural communication, and empowerment are very welcome. Methodological, theoretical, and empirical resources—as well as related anecdotes—would be greatly appreciated.

REFERENCES

Adler, P. (1975). The transitional experience: An alternative view of culture shock. *Journal of Humanistic Psychology, 15*(4), 13–23.

Barber, B. (1992). *An Aristocracy of Everyone: The Politics of Education and the Future of America.* New York: Ballantine.

Berrigan, F. (1981). *Community Communications: The Role of Community Media in Development.* Paris: UNESCO.

Brislin, R. (1981). *Cross-Cultural Encounters: Face to Face Interaction.* New York: Pergamon.

Chaplain's Advisory Committee. (1995). *Report on the Winter Term in Mission Program.* DePauw University.

Church, A. (1982). Sojourner adjustment. *Psychological Bulletin, 91,* 540–575.

Crabtree, R. (1993). *Alternative Development Models: Empowerment and Intercultural Communication in El Salvador.* Paper presented to Society for the Study of Social Problems, August 11–13, Miami, FL.

Freire, P. (1970). *Pedagogy of the Oppressed.* New York: Continuum.

Furnham, A., & Bochner, S. (1986). *Culture Shock.* New York: Methuen.

Hornik, R. (1988). *Development Communication: Information, Agriculture, and Nutrition in the Third World.* New York: Longman.

Martin, J. (1989). Predeparture orientation: Preparing college sojourners for intercultural interaction. *Communication Education, 38,* 249–257.

Nair, K., & White, S. (1987). Participation is the key to development communication. *Media Development, 34*(3), 36–40.

Tandon, R. (1981). Participatory research in the empowerment of people. *Convergence, 14*(3), 20–29.

Wilson, L. Personal interview, April 17, 1995.

3

Confronting the Ultimate Learning Outcome: We Teach Who We Are

Susan Drake

Who you are speaks, speaks so loudly, I can't hear what you're saying.

—Author unknown

We take ourselves with us wherever we go.

—Montaigne

INTRODUCTION

Recently I was asked to be a speaker in a symposium on learning outcomes. The four other speakers focused on shifting responsibility for the outcomes from the teacher to the learner, accompanied with a constructivist view of learning. As I listened I realized that one important aspect was missing from their assertions—the impact of the teacher beyond the cognitive realms. Often I hear people talking about their former teachers and what they did to or with them as if it were happening in the moment. These were clearly formative experiences. For me, in the final analysis, we teach who we are. A teacher's implicit values are very much part of the real lessons of the classroom.

This chapter is an exploration of the understanding of learning outcomes as they are being interpreted in our classrooms today and the role of the teacher in facilitating these outcomes. Three different orientations to outcomes will be examined with their underlying assumptions about what's worth knowing and the relationship between teacher and learner. Finally, the importance of the teacher's being is explored in relationship to learning outcomes.

CURRICULUM ORIENTATIONS AND OUTCOMES

Today, we in the United States are concerned that students are not being prepared in our schools to be productive citizens of the twenty-first century. The focus is on the complex technological and higher-order thinking skills that will be increasingly needed in the workplace. It is already apparent in the workplace that skills that have traditionally been considered the "basics" are no longer enough, and critics claim that even the traditional basics are not being taught well enough. These critics tend to represent business, industry, parents, and some educators; their collective voice has been given prominent attention in the media.

In response to the charges being levied at education, there has been renewed interest in learning outcomes as a route to enhanced learning and increased accountability. But the question still remains: What are students today *really* learning in our classrooms? The dialogue surrounding outcomes still tends to ignore the impact of the hidden curriculum and the unique personality of the teacher who facilitates the delivery of the curriculum. It has long been recognized that the teacher is an important part of the learning outcomes. The good teacher is "a unique human being who has learned to use himself [or herself] effectively and efficiently to carry out his [or her] own and society's purposes in the education of others" (Coombs, Blume, Newman & Wass, 1974, p. 8). This self-as-instrument concept focuses on the teacher as learner who affects the learning.

Over time there has been an evolution in what is considered worth knowing and how learning outcomes have been perceived. Three different orientations to curriculum and their relationship to outcomes are considered here.

Traditional Model

In the late 1950s and 1960s, spurred on by Sputnik and the public perception that we were falling behind the Soviets, the United States underwent an educational crisis very similar to that of today. School reform became a primary objective; educational theorists offered prescriptions for enhanced learning that would allow North Americans to remain competitive. Embedded in these prescriptions was the philosophy that dominated schools at the time, a philosophy that valued efficiency, productivity, and standardization—the factory model. The factory model led to an educational technology that stressed that there existed a most effective "method" for learning.

Many of our schools are still operating under this model where efficiency, method, and standardization are the regulating forces. This model is grounded in technical rationality (Schon, 1983) and procedural knowing (Belenky, Clinchy, Goldberger, & Tarule, 1986). Objectivity and linear thinking characterize accepted ways of knowing such as are found in the scientific method. What is worth knowing are the objective facts. Memorization assured student success.

When the machine metaphor dominates, the emphasis is on the product rather than on the individual (Oliver, 1989). Operating under a factory model, schools evolved into large institutions where learning was separated into subject areas. Students were passive learners exposed to the same content; the teacher delivered the material in a prescribed manner informed by method (Miller, Cassie, & Drake, 1990).

Behavioral objectives became the tool for the teacher to decide exactly what students would learn. Content and activities drove the objectives that teachers developed to organize their teaching units in their subject areas. These objectives were broken down into small manageable parts. For the most part, the objectives were measured by pencil and paper tests. Standardized test scores allowed comparison of students, teachers, schools, regions, states, and even countries.

Yet today we face another educational crisis that suggests this approach to education really doesn't work. The critics call for solving the problem by going back to the basics and the way it used to be. However, others are offering alternative solutions that challenge the epistemological assumptions underlying the traditional model of education. The technology of learning outcomes has shifted in order to be congruent with the epistemological assumptions.

Constructivist Skills Model

A fundamental shift in what's worth knowing is the shift from the acquisition of factual information that can be demonstrated by pencil-and-paper tests to skills that the student will need to be a productive citizen of the future. Typically these skills cross the disciplines and include such things as communication, collaboration, information management, and higher-order thinking skills such as problem solving. These types of outcomes cannot be measured by written tests; they require performance measurement. Educators who assess by performance believe that being able "to do" is parallel to saying that a student has really learned something, rather than simply memorized it. Culminating events or exhibitions are the real test of student learning (Goldberg, 1993).

This perspective is usually identified with constructivism. The student is no longer considered to be an empty vessel passively receiving knowledge. Learning is a process where the learner constructs new meaning within the context of what he or she already knows. This is a developmental process (Miller et al., 1990) where meaning is constructed through transactions between teacher and student. It is here that the student begins to be given some voice in the development of the curriculum.

The tremendous potential of this approach is that it can dramatically change the way a teacher teaches. Providing experiences that lead toward a demonstration can be very different than the traditional delivery of curriculum through textbook and worksheets. A real life context now becomes a prime consideration as teachers try to make both the instructional experiences and the performance assessment authentic. A real-life context moves the teacher into integrating the curriculum. New theories of learning, such as Gardner's (1983) multiple intelligences, demand that there be a wide variety of instructional activities and that not only linguistic and mathematical intelligences be valued. Problem-solving activities are highly valued.

The move toward performance assessment has also included several ongoing measures such as portfolios, journals, interviews, and learning logs. The assumption underlying these is that learning is ongoing and can be optimized by ongoing feedback. This feedback tends to be qualitative in nature and not designed to rank or compare other students.

The constructivist perspective is very different from the traditional model. However, in some ways it is the same. Martin (1985) differentiates between curriculum that honors the productive processes of society and the reproductive processes. For her, the reproductive processes revolve around concern, caring, and connection, whereas the productive processes focus on product. The constructivist skills paradigm is still concerned with product, even though the product is skill demonstration rather than content mastery. In this model it is clear that outcomes must be observable and measurable.

The role of the teacher is acknowledged in this perspective but only in the context of co-constructing meaning for content and skills. The scientific method is the method of choice to solve problems logically and rationally. This is still the realm of procedural thinking. The interconnection of teacher and student as human beings is not considered.

Transformation Model

Theorists offer different names for orientations that extend beyond the constructivist position. For Miller and her colleagues (1990) this is the transformation model where the goal of education is personal growth and social change. Poplin (1988) identifies this orientation by articulating holistic constructivist principles. She stresses the role of affect and intuition as well as the sociopolitical forces in learning. Martin (1985) would consider the reproductive processes to be included here as well as the productive processes. For here there is a place for caring and connection, where becoming "educated can be a journey of integration, not alienation" (p. 83).

The transformation model is inclusive and includes the content and skills that are acquired in the traditional and constructivist models. However, many ways of knowing are legitimized. Subjective knowing is acknowledged. Intuitive thinking is recognized as a complement to procedural knowing. Connected knowing connects experiential knowing with procedural knowing (Belenky et al., 1986). Relational knowing is honored, allowing that a valid and profound way of knowing is through relationships with others (Hollingsworth, 1993). Ontological knowing is knowing with the whole body (Oliver, 1989). Oliver recommends cosmological thinking that explores humanity's place in the universe and to examine qualities of becoming, knowing, participating, and connecting.

How do learning outcomes articulate the highest goals of education? These are called "transformative" or global outcomes and are characteristics named "higher order life skills" (Spady & Marshall, 1991). These include attitudes, intentions, and values such as perseverance, caring, concern for others, flexibility, and social responsibility. For others, these transformative outcomes include wisdom and social change guided by this wisdom (Miller et al., 1990). To me, these transformative outcomes move beyond "doing" to "being" (Drake, 1995).

From the transformative perspective, higher-order life skills offer the fundamental framework for what is worth knowing (Spady & Marshall, 1991). By this theory, all education should be geared toward these higher goals. Spady (1993) recommends that educators design down from the global outcomes when creating curriculum. However, educators who have been trained in the traditional model or even the constructivist skills model have real difficulty with focusing on higher-order life goals as the ultimate learning outcome for students. One problem, of course, revolves around the ambiguity surrounding these life skills and the difficulty of obtaining a precise measurement to indicate how well a student cares or perseveres or whatever. Although these "being" goals are now recognized as important learning outcomes, they usually remain only idealistic goals rather than tangible learning outcomes.

A second problem revolves around the values that are embedded in these life skills. Educators do not seem to question what, for example, it really means to be a productive citizen of the future and the potentially disastrous implications such definitions have for our global village and the environment. Yet, an unquestioned vision of the productive citizen is intended to drive the new learning outcomes technology. We give lip service to the kind of person the educational system produces without really examining the values that we are promoting and what they mean applied in the real world. Recent concern with "character development" indicates an awareness of the "being" aspect of our education. Still, that our assessment tools, whether traditional or performance based, are not able to measure these global or "being" outcomes makes the intended outcomes just so many empty words rather than a focus for learning.

VALUES: TO TEACH OR NOT TO TEACH?

Much of the objection to teaching values in our schools comes from the same critics who claim the system is failing. "Values" do not belong in the classroom. They belong in the homes and churches, where parents can be selective about what values are important to teach. In order not to offend, to appear politically correct, school systems have had to step back from teaching values. Teachers are expected to teach the facts about such volatile issues as AIDS and sex education. However, their own stance while teaching is that of the technician of the traditional model who teaches only facts.

Yet values are taught every day in schools. Although a teacher may not state a position, he or she more often than not has one; students usually want to know the adult's position as a way to compare and make sense of their own. Even if the teacher does not offer his or her perspective on a particular situation, values are being transmitted by what a teacher says and does or by what he or she doesn't say or do. It is impossible to teach a value-free curriculum, for we teach who we are. If students learn nothing else, they can size up and assess and understand the "character" of their teachers extremely quickly. They know who we are and they learn the "being" lessons we teach as we move our way through the structured curriculum.

The "being" aspect of teaching-learning is far beyond recognizing the affective, which is limited to feelings and attitudes; it is about being in the world. Being is rarely directly addressed, yet it is a fundamental part of the school experience occurring at an implicit level. This is the hidden curriculum. In the final analysis, we teach students about "being" in the world by being who we are.

This lesson about being is the ultimate student learning outcome, regardless of grades on a report card or even observable measurable demonstrations occurring in an authentic real-life context.

THEN WHO AM I AND WHAT DO I TEACH?

Given that who we are may be the most important thing that we teach, it seems wise to examine our behaviors to understand the real messages that students are receiving. Fullan (1993) claims that at the core of a good teacher is moral purpose set in the larger social context. As teachers, we must truly care about what is best for the students while moving toward societal improvement. For Fullan, moral requirements include inquiry, knowledge, caring, well-being, freedom, and social justice.

Do we have a moral purpose? Do we teach with heart? Do we really care about the students who have been entrusted to us? For as Noddings (1992) reminds us, students learn skills and content only from teachers they perceive really care about them. As educators we are often saying, "We are doing what's best for the students." But are we? Have we asked these students what they really need and want to learn? Are we really considering their basic needs and how they best learn? Honoring student voices could take many forms, from negotiating the curriculum (Boomer, Lester, Onore, & Cook, 1992; Beane, 1994) to redesigning the architecture of the school according to student input (Taylor, 1993). Often our seemingly well-intentioned attempts at change mean things are easier for the teacher, but perhaps not better for the education of the student.

We can explore our day-to-day behavior to discover the real message we are sending our students. Do we really pay equal attention to genders and to minority groups; or do we, as the literature insists, give more time and attention to white middle-class males (Richmond-Abbott, 1992)? Do we really believe all students can learn and thus structure our lessons to engage all learners in the learning? Do our assessment practices encourage continuous improvement and demonstrate a sincere belief that every student can learn? Do we allow opportunities for students to learn in different modalities, and does our assessment truly honor these modalities? If we believe in "learning by doing," do we create learning environments where this happens?

These types of reflections revolve around tangible teacher behaviors—ones that can be described or measured in some way, and ones that tell a truthful tale about our "espoused" beliefs and values as they compare to our implicit values. Invariably, the student will absorb the implicit value. For many this means, "I am not valued by my teacher. I am not smart enough or good enough." Searching in our memories of our own formative educational experience, we can probably all find evidence of the teacher who did not value or believe in us, and we can understand how truly damaging the consequences of this perception may be.

Embedded in teacher behaviors are the core values we live by. This is the "being" aspect of our curriculum. Although the public demands for educational reform lie largely in the cognitive domain, it is an assumption that our students will be "nice" people at the same time as being productive members of society. A focus on academic excellence alone does not guarantee "nice people," as a look at the Nazi regime informs us. What do we individually teach about being a "nice" person? Do we truly care about our students? Do we demonstrate a respect for all people? Do we behave in ways that respect the environment? Are we flexible? Do we demonstrate perseverance? The list goes on and on. A list without portfolio in most educational circles, but a list that gets to the very heart of teaching.

One dilemma that educators today are facing is how to deal with the exponential increase in human knowledge. Yet we have failed to differentiate between knowledge as in facts and procedures and knowledge about being human. "The knowledge of human beings increases by its height in accumulation, while knowledge of being human increases by the depth of its penetration (Young & Gehrke, 1993). Working within the transformative paradigm, teachers need more than a change of theoretical framework; they need a change of heart that incorporates the unity and coherence of being (Smith, 1982).

The questions we must ask become the big questions of life: Who am I? What is the meaning and purpose of my life? How can I live out this purpose in my life? These are the same questions our students must wrestle with—questions that they thirst to explore. Do we provide opportunities to explore these questions, or are we focused exclusively on the acquisition of facts and/or skills? Do we ask these questions of ourselves?

In many ways the transformation model is about making connections. The implicit assumption is that reality is interconnected and interdependent. Jennings (1994) suggests that education should give students experience in understanding this reality. It should allow students to develop a sense of global connection with others. It is only with this deep understanding of being part of a larger reality that they can then answer the big questions in ways that honor themselves, others, and the planet.

Entering the transformative world, the teacher values alternative ways of knowing. The student constructs meaning not only through the logical, linear side of knowing but also through the intuitive side—subjective knowing through metaphor, story, and symbol. These types of strategies become the hallmark of a transformational curriculum such as the Story Model (Drake et al., 1992). We learn by making connections (Caine & Caine, 1991). Making connections—whether across subject areas, from the whole to the part, or to our own personal stories—optimizes the way our brains work to make meaning of the world.

Moving beyond reflection to being, teachers can take these journeys themselves by exploring such things as story image and metaphor (Drake & Miller, 1991). As well, Miller in *The Holistic Teacher* (1993) and *The Contemplative Practitioner* (1994) offers practical strategies, such as meditation and slowing down, whereby a teacher can reflect on the meaning of his or her life. These strategies go beyond critical reflection of one's classroom behaviors. They get to the core of our being by stripping away the espoused values to reveal who we really are. They also help the practitioner to understand, at an experiential level, how the professional and personal are deeply interconnected. Miller's point is that by engaging in a life of balance between head and heart and body and mind, educators can begin to find the real meaning of existence itself. Here we can discover and be guided by the "big Self" within each of us.

CONCLUSION

The real crisis today is much deeper than an educational crisis where students are not learning the skills necessary to be produc-

Figure 3.1
Redefined Learning Outcomes

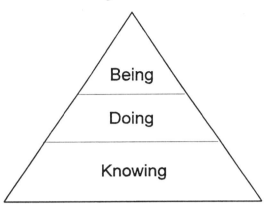

tive citizens of the future. The real crisis is a moral and spiritual crisis (Purpel, 1989), one that is reflected in every aspect of our society today from family breakdown, increased violence, drug use, health care, abuse cases, and oppression of minority groups to the erosion of organized religion. We no longer have our core values to guide us. Moffett (1994) recommends a spiritual curriculum that will promote a lifelong spiritual quest to become the best human being one can be.

However, most of us teach in schools where openly spiritual curricula are suspect. How can we continue to teach and honor the things we hold dear? I have used a diagram (Figure 3.1) to help people make meaning of today's outcomes in ways that honor their deepest beliefs. This diagram is a modification of Spady's (1994) outcome demonstration mountain.

Spady recommends that we design down from the higher order life skills when we are developing curriculum. Yet these skills are rarely ones that are easily measured and fall into the "being" realm. Teachers can plan by focusing up toward the type of person that they wish the students to be. First, they need to make explicit the characteristics that they wish to see in students—characteristics such as caring, compassion, service to others, and caring for the environment. With these characteristics always in mind, the doing and knowing (skills and knowledge) can be planned to guide a young person in this direction. In this way, the teacher has articulated a moral purpose that is set in a larger social context.

If we are truly to educate students to be productive citizens of the future, we need them to be responsible, caring citizens regardless of the academic content stuffed into their heads. According to Michael Fullan, "teachers today have a real chance to reshape the profession for the future—an opportunity that rarely comes along" (Shaw & Beattie, 1994, p. 8). As teachers, we make a significant contribution to the "character" of each student we teach. This can happen in two ways. First, although new influences such as educational technology may seem mechanistic, they can be applied in ways that begin this process if we focus on the "being" aspect within all learning activities we plan. Second, we must commit to practice what we preach. Modeling has always been a powerful teacher. It is time we confronted the ultimate learning outcome and became accountable for what we teach about being in the world.

REFERENCES

Beane, J. (1994, January). *Curriculum integration problems: Possibilities and politics.* Second Annual National Conference on Curriculum Integration, Scottsdale, AZ.

Belenky, M., Clinchy, B., Goldberger, N., & Tarule, J. (1986). *Women's ways of knowing: The development of self, voice, and mind.* New York: Basic Books.

Boomer, G., Lester, N., Onore, C., & Cook, J. (Eds.). (1992). *Negotiating the curriculum: Educating for the 21st century.* London: Falmer Press.

Caine, R. N., & Caine, G. (1991). *Making connections: Teaching and the human brain.* Alexandria: VA: Association for Supervision and Curriculum Development.

Coombs, A. W., Blume, R., Newman, A., & Wass, H. (1974). *The professional education of teachers: A humanistic approach to teacher preparation.* Boston: Allyn & Bacon.

Drake, S. (1995) Connecting the learning outcomes to integrated curriculum. *Orbit, 26*(1), 28–32.

Drake, S. M., Bebbington, J., Laksman, S., Mackie, P., Maynes, N., & Wayne, L. (1992). *Developing an integrated curriculum using the Story Model.* Toronto: OISE Press.

Drake, S. M., & Miller, J. P. (1991). Beyond reflection to being: The contemplative practitioner. *Phenomenology and Pedagogy. 9*, 319–334.

Fullan, M. (1993). *The change forces.* London: Falmer Press.

Gardner, H. (1983). *Frames of mind*. New York: Basic Books.

Goldberg, M. (1993). A portrait of Ted Sizer. *Educational Leadership*. 5(1), 53–56.

Hollingsworth, S. (1993, July). *Relational knowing and collaborative processes*. Presentation at Brock University, St. Catherines, ON.

Jennings, T. (1994). Self-in-connection as an component of human rights advocacy and education. *Journal of Moral Education*. 23(3), 285–296.

Martin, J. (1985). Becoming educated: A journey of alienation or integration. *Journal of Education, 167* (3), 71–84

Miller, J. P. (1993). *The holistic teacher*. Toronto: OISE Press.

Miller, J. P. (1994). *The contemplative practitioner*. Westport, CT: Bergin & Garvey

Miller, J. P., Cassie, B., & Drake, S. M. (1990). *Holistic learning: A teacher's guide to integrated studies*. Toronto: OISE Press.

Moffett, J. (1994). *The universal schoolhouse*. San Francisco, CA: Jossey-Bass.

Noddings, N. (1992). *The challenge to care in schools*. New York: Teachers College Press.

Oliver, D. (1989). *Education, modernity, and fractured meaning: Toward a process theory of teaching and learning*. New York: SUNY Press.

Poplin, M. (1988). Holistic/Constructivist principles of the teaching/learning process: Implications for the field of learning disabilities. *Journal of Learning Disabilities, 21*(7), 401–416.

Purpel, D. E. (1989). *The moral and spiritual crisis in education*. South Hadley, MA: Bergin & Garvey.

Richmond-Abbott, M. (1992). *Masculine & feminine: Gender roles in the life cycle*. New York: McGraw-Hill.

Schon, D. (1983). *The reflective practitioner*. New York: Basic Books.

Shaw, P., & Beattie, M. (1994). Conceptualizing the teacher's role: An Interview with Michael Fullan. *Orbit, 25*(4), 6–8.

Smith, H. (1982) *Beyond the postmodern mind*. Wheaton, IL: Theosophical Publishing.

Spady, W. (1993, December). *All about learning outcomes*. Annual Ontario Secondary School Teachers' Federation Conference, Toronto.

Spady, W. (1994). "Choosing outcomes of significance." *Educational Leadership, 51*(6), 18–22.

Spady, W., & Marshall, K. (1991). "Beyond traditional outcome-based education." *Educational Leadership, 49*(2), 67–72.

Taylor, A. (1993) "How schools are redesigning their space." *Educational Leadership, 51*(1), 36–41.

Young, D., & Gehrke, N. (1993). "Curriculum integration for transcendence: A critical review of recent books on curriculum for integration." *Curriculum Inquiry, 23*(4), 445–454.

4

Transforming School Psychology: Paradigmatic Assumptions and Impediments to Holistic Roles

Dudley J. Wiest and Dennis A. Kreil

INTRODUCTION

"School Psychology is a psychological specialty with multiple roles and functions—a complex profession that demands flexibility and clinical acumen" (Reynolds, Gutkin, Elliot, & Witt, 1984). Anyone who has practiced in the field of school psychology for several years or more realizes that the definition of job function for school psychologists that Reynolds and colleagues proposed in 1984 is *not* an overstatement. Their denotation of a school psychologist's function minimally describes the complexity that surrounds this field specialty. In fact, suggesting that school psychology is a specialty (in the singular sense) is really inaccurate and paradoxical, since intervention from this capacity immediately casts the helper into many simultaneous roles such as consultant, assessor, therapist, parent educator, facilitator, administrator, social worker, liaison, politician, advocate, researcher, and instructor. These compounding job roles are often necessary and yet can be quite conflicting in time and system requirements.

Various school systems, dependent upon the district and area of the country that dictates the values and needs of the institution, typically demand more or less time in any one domain. Thus, the individual school psychologist continues to have a narrow definition of job role. To compound this issue, the dominant legal structure is even more confining in the execution of job roles by the school psychologist.

In spite of these pressures, school psychologists have a certain degree of freedom in performing their vocational roles. However, individual choice in the execution of job role is not always a salutary perspective, for if the psychologist does not have a philosophical grounding and orientation that is consistent, the pulls and demands of service may create a dissonance and skew delivery of service into directions that are antithetical to appropriate children's intervention. Hence, there needs to be an "orientation process" within the district system, where the various levels of human structure agree what their mission is, what they believe that means in the delivery of service and instruction, and the consequent allocation of funding and time to comply with their beliefs. Individual service delivery then evolves from this mutual set of beliefs that all members agree represent their system. This is not to supersede the federal law, which the larger cultural system has deemed representative of our beliefs. Rather, the local district and state missions should be grounded in the larger, cultural, legal requirements that depict our national value system. In turn, great effort must be exerted to ensure that the national mission for children is clear and representative of what our culture and society promulgate.

Theoretically, this would seem a reasonable approach to the craft of a school psychologist. In practice, the ability to integrate such logic is often difficult to put into application. Creating a consensus on law, service delivery, and the coordination of various disciplines such as speech and language therapy, occupational-physical therapy, visual, hearing, and mobility training, vocational training, and teaching-instruction in special education defies the well-intentioned attempts of coordinating a program of intervention. This is not to imply that programs are poorly run and inadequate; rather, the task of integrating the specialties is complex, difficult, and dynamic in scope, particularly when multiple models and beliefs regarding children exist among disciplines. To complicate this equation, school psychology is, as is the larger system of culture, a system in the midst of dynamic change.

Society and its subsystems are not only ripe for change; they are exploding with change. Therefore, the theme of this chapter is change—in essence, reformation of an educational subsystem, namely, school psychology. After reviewing relevant themes of change that have recently come to the forefront for education in general and school psychology specifically, a paradigm will be presented to frame change and service delivery for school psychology. A set of organizational impediments to positive change will be introduced, with recommendations for a positive transformation into new job roles for school psychologists.

TRANSITION IN THE 1980S

As a whole, public education was criticized in the past decade for its failure to address student needs that are considered crucial for the learning process to occur. Goodlad (1984) found inequity in the access to quality knowledge and pedagogical practices, suggesting that methods such as the tracking of youngsters according to ability and achievement levels actively blocked their admission to systems of higher learning and subsequent jobs. In addition, he cited the lack of praise and correction of a student's performance, the paucity of interaction in classrooms, the narrow range of activities utilized in the learning process (e.g., listening to teachers, answering question, and taking tests) and the lack of time allocated to students for subject comprehension as pivotal liabilities in the education programs of over 1,000 classrooms.

Glasser (1990) estimated that fewer than 15 percent of those who attend school do quality work. He attributed this striking statistic of underachievement to the management style most often employed in schools. Students learn best and contribute optimally to the learning process when they have teachers who utilize noncoercive techniques of instruction. Unfortunately, coercive teachers are considered the norm and thus impair internal needs such as survival, love, power, fun, and freedom. Students are relegated to the status of workers who are passively expected to conform, oftentimes establishing an adversarial, noncollaborative environment.

Thus, schools should be places where teaching is contextually oriented and the teacher-student relationship is more egalitarian than authoritative. Students then transform from externally manipulated objects to active subjects who critically examine the world (Shor, 1980).

McLaren (1989) suggested that schools reflect a set of ideals from the culture at large and consequently are not value-free. Teachers are encouraged to examine their own instructional pedagogical practices to uncover their hidden ideological interests. This "critical pedagogy" analytically examines schools historically and in the current social and political context so that common biases are confronted. The assumption is that equal opportunities are not provided to the underclass, poor, minority, and female from the dominant white male culture biases inherent within our education system. Consequently, school motivation and achievement can be framed as how effectively the educational system values trust between students and faculty, recognizes students' personal legitimacy as human beings, and provides opportunity to obtain a positive economic status (Erickson, 1987). Resistance (i.e., refusal to learn) by students occurs when there is a stereotyped ethnic or social class identity that is assigned to a group or school. There is little trust or sense of respect for the students.

Griffin (1988) studied average youngsters who did not work to their potential during high school. The cohort was not represented by either dropouts or delinquents (those with acting-out behavior). The schools were viewed as needing to "slow down, scale down, personalize, and democratize" (p. 263). There were too many students to develop a sense of identity, students had difficulty being personally known, too many topics were expected to be mastered daily, and little emphasis was placed on empowering students to make choice and decisions.

Not all students simply choose to underachieve when confronted with a system that is rigid and inflexible in its pedagogy. The national rate for high school dropouts is around 25 percent (Fine, 1991; Goodlad, 1984), and adolescents are in a sense "provoked" to act out through misbehavior.

Scholastic failure seems to increase the likelihood of delinquent behavior such as truancy, smoking, theft, insubordination, and selling drugs. Personal failure experiences in school threaten the student's self-esteem. To raise self-esteem, youngsters rebel in delinquent acts. Students who perceive a more flexible set of rules in school , whether they are in alternative or regular education programs, gain more academic competence and are more committed to their roles as students. Grades improve and the need to exhibit delinquency diminishes (Gold & Mann, 1987).

The academic failure experiences are particularly influential when emanating from negative episodes that occur as early as first grade. Problems such as delayed reading, learning disabilities, illness, and multiple moves were typical of high-risk students from an alternative education high school who were unwilling to learn in spite of a specialized curriculum and counseling that were implemented with the assistance of students from the school. Apathy, drug and/or alcohol use, conflict with peers, family friction, and a sense of futility were common factors related to unwilling students' behaviors (Bobo, 1987).

Fine's (1991) ethnographic study of urban public high schools concluded that institutional practices and ideologies "silence" the voices of students and effectively encourage students either to drop out or to be discharged (removed) from the site. Silencing occurs by sarcasm, humiliating statements, competition between students and practices that disallow discussion and dialogue. In addition to the silencing of students' voices, teachers feel disempowered and professionally deprived of support, encouragement, and a voice in policy. As disempowerment for educators rises, the rationalization for faculty belief systems that are damaging to pupils also rises. Fine stresses the need for transformative policies that accentuate empowering faculties, interdisciplinary curriculum reflective of indigenous cultures, and commitment to listening to subgroups, whether they be students, teachers, administrators, or parents.

Recently the Institute for Transformation in Education (1992) reported findings from qualitative research of people who work inside the schools. Fundamental problems in relationships, cultural sensitivity, values, teaching, safety, physical environment, and despair contribute to symptoms such as low achievement and high dropout rates. Again, it is the culture of school that must be examined to adequately explore and discover positive solutions for the ills of students.

In summary, schools have been assailed in recent years as places that are rigid, inflexible, inadequately instructed, and poorly managed. Instruction has been encouraged to become more contextual and democratic, with the school system critically examining its own pedagogy and inherent biases. Transformation is advocated to ameliorate resistance, delinquency, underachievement, and dropping out.

THE CALL FOR CHANGE IN SCHOOL PSYCHOLOGY

Various authors have promoted the need for change in education in the past decade; leaders in school psychology also paralleled this dynamic, calling for reformation of service delivery and intervention for children. During the 1980s the field of school psychology labored over the issue of transition to a more productive and viable set of service goals, corresponding job roles, and appropriate intervention practices.

School psychology faced two simultaneous drives that pressured the change process. Services were expected to expand and become more comprehensive in scope for all children. At the same time, reductionistic legal requirements of the special education law were mandated and had to be adhered to. These legalistic requisites were often viewed as incongruent with how psychologists conceptualize learning and development (Bardon, 1987). In essence, Public Law 94-142 (renamed IDEA: Individuals with Disabilities Education Act), which guaranteed free and appropriate education for all children, had become an asset as much as a detriment for school psychologists. Although it created new jobs and allowed personnel to become more proficient at roles such as assessment, it restricted *practice* opportunities (e.g., counseling and consultation) by creating a rigid framework for conceptualizing learning problems. A "medical model" was institutionalized, reducing daily interventions to their most basic, mechanistic forms: diagnosis and assessment. A dissonance was created between actual work lives and potential skills which could be employed. Underutilization of skills emerged in the struggle to conform to the strict maintenance of the law (Bardon, 1987). School psychologists spent over 50 percent of the professional day in assessment despite the desire of most psychologists to be more proactive and interventive in their roles (Benson & Hughes, 1985). There evolved a discrepancy between desired roles and actual roles. Ironically, the training for school psychologists before Public Law 94-142 was much more supportive of job roles beyond intelligence testing, such as consultation, parent training, and intervention (Anderson, Brown, & Hohenshil, 1984).

Problematically, the phenomenon of *refer-test-place*—children are referred to special education, tested, and in most instances, placed in a remedial program—proved to be ineffective. The services of such programs simply did not demonstrate competence, yet they demanded time to implement for the school psychologist. Compounding the issue, staff at school sites—the consumers of school psychology services—perceived traditional roles of assessment to be salutary and wanted additional time carrying out those functions (Abel & Burke, 1985).

Hence, rigidly adhering to a "refer, test, and place" dynamic promoted several problems in service to children. First, this approach was flawed and did not effectively help children in the way it was proposed and designed to do. There was a lack of continuity between identification of students and subsequent programs to service children (Shin, 1986). Second, many children identified as handicapped were in fact not disabled. Irrelevant labels were used in a deficit-driven categorization that was arbitrarily defined, and regular education subsequently abdicated its role in flexibly educating children (Graden, Zins, & Curtis, 1988). Third, many of the concerns about adjustment and learning for children could be addressed in a preventative rather than reactive manner (Zins & Forman, 1988). Finally, burnout among school psychologists was greatest among those who had a focus on assessment activities (Huberty & Buebner, 1988).

In response to such concerns, various authors have proffered solutions that address a more thorough response to children in need. The National Association of School Psychologists (NASP) increased its political body and influence as policy-setting group advocating children's services. Maturing as a political force, it has focused on school psychologists working more in regular education than in distinctly special education, attempting to promote alternative services for *all* children (Fagan, 1989). By investing energy and resources into the belief that all children can learn, inappropriate placements into special education will be lessened (Graden et al., 1988). In addition, support for higher purposes of human development such as autonomy, self-actualization, and social responsibility are advocated as imperative needs for children (Hart, 1989).

Many of the referrals for children who exhibit learning and emotional adjustment problems can be addressed in a preventative manner, emphasizing coping skills training, cognitive education strategies, social resistance, parenting classes, media programs, peer counseling, family planning, coordination with mental health agencies, and peer tutoring (Zins & Forman, 1988).

One such preventative approach, entitled "neverstreaming," is employed within a school district to keep children out of special education. The school and community blend resources systematically to keep students from becoming academically handicapped. Using credentialed teachers who tutor children daily and provide family support, the program never placed into special education 90 percent of children identified as "at risk" (Slavin et al., 1991).

A preventative approach dictates the need for more indirect service roles from school psychologists (Stewart, 1986). Not only must psychologists transition to a more idiographic and ecologically sensitive system of assessment (Fuchs & Fuchs, 1986); but it is recommended that in the schools they employ a consultant-based approach for intervention that is ecologically sensitive and incorporates various aspects of a child's life (Reynolds et al., 1984). In the present decade school psychology will ideally emphasize more prereferral intervention, curriculum-based assessment, and behavioral intervention through a consultative model (Pfeiffer & Dean, 1988), although current research indicates that the encouragement for deemphasis on assessment remains ignored (Hutton, Dubes, & Muir, 1992).

MOVING TO A HOLISTIC PARADIGM

In essence, what various leaders of school psychology are promoting, without being specific, is a paradigm shift. The numerous suggestions and admonishments for transition are fruitless unless a common metatheory serves as a grounding force for specific models of service. This metatheory provides the impetus for making the difficult organizational decisions that are necessary for the determination of specific job roles. In essence, organizations cannot run effectively unless they acknowledge what are the underlying values, thoughts, and perceptions of reality that are endemic within the culture. It is the values, thoughts, and perceptions that make up the cultural paradigm and thus influence every subsequent decision that emanates from the culture.

Note that the concept of paradigm is more than simply a theory. A paradigm is a way of seeing the world (Heshusius, 1989). Action in the world is secondary to the paradigm. As such, there is not a prescription for skills within the science of holism. Rather, techniques and procedures derive from the world view of holism.

Capra (1982) described the scientific evolution from a mechanistic, Newtonian paradigm to an organismic, holistic view of life. This shift originated in the hard sciences, particularly in the area of physics, with scientists such as Einstein, Heisenberg, and Bohm supporting the transition to a holistic conceptualization and philosophy of life (Russell, 1983).

Definitively, holism is a systems view of life, where the whole of the system is more than the sum of the parts and not explainable by the parts. The system is nonlinear, complex, self-organizing, always open, and exchanging matter with its environment. Behavior is determined by a dynamic interaction of many variables (Heshusius, 1982). These systems that comprise reality are integrated wholes whose properties cannot be reduced to those of smaller units. They are flexible in nature, process oriented, adaptable, and actively governed by a dynamic known as transaction, the simultaneous and mutually interdependent interaction between multiple components (Capra, 1982).

Various authors in education have advocated the need for such a paradigm shift (Heshusius, 1982, 1986, 1989; Poplin, 1987, 1988a, 1988b), and holism is gradually replacing the mechanistic paradigm, which has shaped much of special education (Heshusius, 1982). Holistic approaches to teaching and intervention are emerging in the areas of literacy and reading (Weaver, 1985), writing (DuCharme, Earl, & Poplin, 1989), the learning process of all children (Poplin, 1988b), attention deficit–hyperactivity disorder (Wiest & Stone, 1993), service delivery for school psychologist (Wiest, 1991), and learning disabilities (Rhodes & Dudley-Marling, 1988), with specific emphasis on nontraditional talents (Stone, Poplin, Johnson, & Simpson, 1992) and divergent thinking and feeling (Stone, Poplin, Johnson, & Simpson, 1991). In addition, leadership within the field of school psychology is beginning to urge that a more holistic orientation be applied to the schools (Hart, 1987; *NASP Communique*, 1992). Application of holistic principles to service delivery for children is varied and could include such areas as child development, family-school intervention, and assessment.

A DEVELOPMENTAL OR SYSTEMS APPROACH

Bronfenbrenner (1979) proposed that development is a permanent change within the individual that results from the mutual accommodation with the environment. He suggested that the environment includes more than the immediate setting and includes the microsystem (e.g., home, school, or church), mesosystem (connection between systems), exosystem (system that does not *directly* involve the developing person but its policies and decisions influence the development, such as a school board), and macrosystem (ideology and belief system of the culture). These systems are interconnected in a nested fashion, with the macrosystem subsuming all other systems. This holistic model of development can then be incorporated within a framework for systems intervention by the school psychologist (Anderson, 1983). Children are viewed within a broader context of their presenting needs, and the behavior is conceptualized as multi-influential and reciprocal.

Employing a holistic paradigm with the intervention work of children necessitates the involvement of families. Consultation with home and school thus becomes a cornerstone of intervention, and the focus on child psychopathology becomes secondary to understanding behavior within the context of multiple environments and influences (see West and Idol, 1987, for an analysis of ten consultation models that may be used with children). Interpretations are "reframed" from blaming the child to understanding contexts and creating solutions (Fine, 1991). The emphasis transcends from "why" a child behaves in such a manner to "how" a family or school interacts with a child (Dowling & Osborne, 1985). Family and school patterns can be analyzed for the degree of positive boundaries and communication that are displayed between systems (Power & Bartholomew, 1987).

Assessing a child holistically requires that emphasis on non-medical, nonmechanistic forms of gathering data be employed. A child's strengths rather than weaknesses should be accentuated, with a focus on problem solving instead of pathology. For example, examination of the family subsystems (Paget, 1987) and various ecologies of the student (Paget & Nagle, 1986) accentuate data collection systemically and provide a totally different path for hypothesis formulation and problem resolution. Assessment is framed within the context of examining children within their various ecologies and cultural milieus. Neurological impairment and specific disabilities are secondary to understanding social context and norms.

In sum, the field of school psychology is beginning to understand that children are best served through a holistic lens of interpretation. Such a view accentuates prevention, consultation, ecology, and the positive strengths of human beings. It is our position that the majority of school psychologists want to change from legal, reductionistic roles and assumptions to more holistic interventions. However, while some colleagues have examined and transformed their beliefs and service roles, many others remain loyal to reductionistic roles of assessment and intervention. Based upon previous research (Wiest & Kreil, 1995), we hypothesize that there exists a series of systemic barriers that inhibit and often prevent the transition to a more holistic paradigm for many practicing school psychologists.

IMPEDIMENTS TO A HOLISTIC VIEW AND SERVICE

The field of special education is hampered in the quest for a holistic transformation. There are four theme areas that blend together as impediments mitigating against a holistic, constructivistic view of education. These areas include the impact of the legal system, rigid beliefs, asystemic thinking, and time constraints. These four dimensions reflect the obstruction to holism because of their grounding in a more mechanistic framework (Wiest & Kreil, in press). These issues also daily affect the role of school psychologists and influence the thinking and conceptualization of student problems. It is the impact of such factors that in essence creates the dissonance between what a school psychologist may "want to do" and feels "compelled to do." Thus, we envision the school psychologist as a professional who often has to transition between two very divergent worlds: the world of linear, medical, and behavioristic thinking and the world of global, interconnected, systemic thinking. Metaphorically, it is akin to walking around with one's foot stuck in a bucket, for the balancing of two worldviews is awkward, time consuming, and wearying. Each of these world system viewpoints has specific expectations about roles. Often these roles are incongruous and create what we conceptualize as "role diffusion," the splitting and scattering of one's function and vocational capacity. This troublesome balance results from our overemphasis on the legal structure in schools, particularly special education, lack of understanding by parents and professionals about a systemic viewpoint, rigid belief systems by parents and professionals, and the simple lack of time to address both worldviews.

The Role of the Law

Laws such as IDEA and section 504 of the Rehabilitation code are created by members of our society in the hope of establishing a framework of justice for individuals and groups within the culture. It is assumed that the litigators are responsible citizens who have a clear focus for justice and are not merely influenced by powerful lobby groups. These laws however are imperfect and vulnerable to misinterpretations and overgeneralizations by those using the statutes. In addition, a law is only as valid as the thinking of the political group that had the power to implement its existence.

School psychologists are well aware of the impact of law. Although school psychology has long been involved in education, the job roles of school psychology have transitioned according to the legal influences upon special education in general. The legal parameters of special education are so rigid that joining the various systems with which children are daily connected is very difficult.

We see the school psychologist as a natural facilitator for mediating children's needs and operating as an integration agent between home, and classroom, playground, community, and any other system within which the child operates. Unfortunately, parents', advocates', teachers', and administrators' overemphasis on legal mandates for assessment, identification, and placement has created a rather narrow and restrictive role of leadership for school psychologists.

In addition, many school psychologists within the field lack consensus about their roles. The "legal" connection to the assessment process in special education law creates an artificial sense of job security and dependence upon safe and predictable assessment roles. Assessment, programming for special education (IEP), and report writing become the hallmark of intervention. Primarily, this role is to comply with the law. What is noteworthy about that logic is the absence of an intervention philosophy. In other words, thinking about how to help children, whether it be in prevention, intervention, or crisis, is secondary to upholding legal mandates.

We concede that legal parameters may be necessary to enforce a justice orientation for certain children in schools. Litigation would not be necessary if our culture—specifically the field of education—could develop some consensus about how to demonstrate the commitment to ensuring appropriate education for all students. The likelihood of developing a consensus without legal prescription appears unlikely in the near future.

However, primarily addressing the needs of children through the legal lens has serious consequences. Parents who are focused on the legal process fail to see the "whole" of the child's experience. Operationally, the child is defined by goals and objectives, and the intuitive, creative, spiritual domain of the child is absent from consideration. In addition, as Coles (1987) noted, many childhood problems such as learning disabilities and attention disorders are grounded in the organization of the family system. Diagnosis for individual disorders are overpathologized and underconceptialized.

Parents who are so focused upon the adherence to legal proceedings may be responding to rigid school structures and thus take a more bellicose stance as a way of penetrating the system norms. Naturally, this lacks the systemic groundedness to address concerns about children effectively, but the dynamic does create a minimal structure to address childhood matters.

It is understandable why certain parents would turn to the law as a way of resolving conflict with rigid school systems. Certain school systems appear to be paralyzed, unyielding, and unresponsive to the needs of children and subsequent concerns of parents, forcing the parents to receive assistance through legal directives. What is less clear is why various parents respond to school systems in a threatening and punitive manner when there has been no overt school system provocation. Unwittingly, the law occasionally becomes a tool to punish even the most responsive and cooperative staff by individuals who misperceive legal intention, overlook or misunderstand how the school is intervening, or lack personal insight into their own problems and thus project their parental responsibility onto the schools.

Family representatives are not alone in the over reliance upon legal structures to address concerns of children. The education establishment is often guilty of the same transgression. Teachers and administrators who perceive the child in terms of behavioral guidelines fail to truly understand the child. Strengths of the child, different styles of learning and cognitions, and ecological "goodness of fit" are subordinate to the concerns of fifty-day timelines, fair-hearing threats, IEPs, and placating parents.

School psychologists feel a great deal of pressure to adhere to a strict interpretation of the law. This creates both a primary pattern and a secondary pattern of interaction for the school psychologist. The school psychologist's initial response to legal mandates, particularly when he or she is made accountable for actions in legal proceedings, is to stop considering the child and begin to consider the domain of the law. Thus, systemic thinking for child advocacy diminishes and linear responses to the law begins. The secondary result is a pattern of gradually adhering to the law as a norm, even when the threat of legal retribution by parents and advocates is no longer predominant. In essence, school psychologists and school teams are put on trial for their violation of the law and eventually become slaves to it. The end result is suspicion between home and school, rigid behavior to adhere to legal mandates, and loss of focus upon the interconnected nature of the child.

Thinking Systemically

If one accepts the world and reality as holistic and organismic in structure, then it is not difficult to conceive of daily experiences as transitioning from system to system. Each interaction by a human thus involves the entrance, association, and departure from one system to the next system. Each system, with its integrated subsystems that cannot be reduced to individual parts, has its own specific rules and norms.

School psychologists are hampered in their mission to address the needs of the student holistically when various constituents from the child's systems do not acknowledge the interconnected nature of the child's ecological experience. Although a school psychologist can advocate for a systemic or ecological conceptualization of childhood development and behavior, one member's paradigmatic orientation cannot create the unity necessary to assist the child.

We suggest that school staffs need to begin to recognize the many ecological dimensions a family experiences. In addition, we also propose that families and their advocates acknowledge the various systemic elements that are inherent within the school environment.

Families are very complex entities, often evolving with cross-generational norms for behavior. They are heterogeneous, and it is no longer advantageous to conceptualize them as simply having a mother, father, and children. Exceptions to the traditional family system include step-families, single-parent families, families in which grandparents raise the children, gay and lesbian families, extended family members in the household, and families with adult children living at home. Families need a tremendous amount of support, especially if one parent is assuming the primary parenting role. Transportation, day care, jobs that pay a decent wage, affordable housing, emotional support from community and school, safety, recreational opportunities for children, and strong schools are a few of the areas parents believe are important for the development of their children.

Schools are also multisystemic in scope and function best when parents understand the various pressures and system demands that are intrinsic to the organization. This is not to excuse poor interactions with parents but to create a framework of understanding how such complicated systems can creatively respond to a family.

School systems are hierarchical in nature, with local city districts subsumed under the ordinances and structures of federal, state, and even county affiliations. Highly political bodies, local school boards are influential in shaping the norms of the district. The central administrative power structure constructs many of the local school site norms through its directives. Local school policy is shaped by the faculty, administrative support team such as principal, school psychologist, and counselor; community advisory boards; and various other systems such as central office, county, state, and federal government. All these structures coalesce policy into the local school norm and procedure.

Regrettably, the system that subsumes all other systems and creates the context of our cultural norms (macrosystem) appears to lack a clear transition into a holistic perspective. Our culture's focus on independence instead of interdependence may undercut many families, leaving schools somehow to provide what we are culturally unwilling to do. Schools feed children, sometimes assist with clothing, provide values and moral training, and also carry out the primary mission of training children in the thinking process our culture deems imperative for survival. Our culture's focus on the independent mentality of our members discourages a unity and care for all people. In essence, the result is intervention for a disability or behavior as opposed to prevention through a care orientation that acknowledges our interconnectedness. Drug babies, homeless children, hungry children, high infant mortality rates, high rates of depression and suicide, proliferation of divorce, rising murder rates, and existential ennui point to a disdain of holistic conceptualization in culture that ultimately affects schools, since they are in fact interconnected.

Rigid Belief Systems

School psychologists operate as agents of change for the benefit of children. They attempt to intervene within the school system directly, as well as to create a broader systemic change within the wider influence of culture. Often rigid belief systems from the educational and home structures thwart efforts to create optimal environments for children.

School systems frequently employ mechanistic beliefs that deter the process of merging home and school into a synergetic alliance for the child. Children are often defined by the set of curricular goals and objectives constructed to measure learning. These defined skills are typically hierarchical, seldom taking into account learner differences and variant interests. A student's problems are ascribed to deficiency within the child. In essence, that a child is struggling with a discreet set of material is blamed on some deficit within that child. This kind of inflexible belief system does not take into account learner styles, temperament, decontextualized curriculum, incongruent instructional technique, and other classroom explanations for lack of school success. These beliefs also imply a lack of competence by educational staff. Children conceptualized as deficient or neurologically impaired are assumed to require attention beyond the classroom teacher's expertise. Although this may be true in some cases, this belief often impedes a systems approach to problem solving.

Blame for lack of school mastery also transcends the child. School staffs may blame parents and culture for academic and social problems within the school. When a child struggles to learn, families are scrutinized for deficiencies. Dual-working-parent families, single-parent families, low- income families, uneducated families, and minority families are identified as deficiency factors. Although these family arrangements may in some way contribute to problems in learning and adjustment, they seldom explain the intricacies of behavior.

Families may also disrupt the merging of systems by holding faulty beliefs. When their children have problems, families may conceptualize their child as disabled before there is data to support such an assumption. In essence, they support the cultural supposition that learning problems emanate from a medical, neurological condition that can be ameliorated only by special education. If schools do not agree, they are to be mistrusted. Hence, adversarialism becomes the belief for amelioration of the childhood weakness.

Such faulty beliefs create a circular set of beliefs between systems. When schools blame parents or parents blame schools for problems the child displays, the other party reacts defensively, which reinforces the belief. Both parties then become mistrustful and fail to merge systems. The solution is, in essence, to blame the other party, leading to no solution.

School psychologists are typically thrust in the awkward role of mediating such fixed beliefs of educators and parents. Until the various members of a child's ecology view behavior through the lens of systemic influence, the child is "medically impaired" and unable to succeed because of the internal handicap.

Lack of Time

The field of school psychology is presented with an occupational dilemma. Reforming and restructuring the profession demands that the individual practitioner become more holistic in the approach to understanding children and their families. As such, child development is considered within the structure of a systems model, emphasizing various interconnected levels of interactions between parts to create the whole of an organism. Thus, the behavior of students is conceptualized as being influenced from a variety of system components such as family orientation, culture, school climate, type of teacher, and community.

The paradox for school psychologists is that even though reformers want an ecological and systems perspective of children and their behavior, legal mandates, reflective of a pathological and reductionistic nature of children's behavior, dictate much of what the psychologist must do. The "refer-test-place" model is still predominant as an intervention for school problems in children. Hence, the roles that reformers want school psychologists to employ and the roles which are necessary to comply with the legal structure of special education are converse.

To conceptualize children's behavior systemically suggests a change to a consultative format. It is crucial for representatives from the child's various subsystems to gather and collectively address the concerns and collaboratively develop some interventions. Changing curriculum, teaching approaches, home-school organization, family dynamics, and classroom culture are just a few of the possible ways to reframe the difficulty from residing within the child to representing mismatches between the child and the ecology. Parents and educators may hail the salutary benefits of consultation and a more holistic approach. However, the most typical result is the desire by parents or educators to have *both* models employed.

In sum, holistic school psychologists operate within two conflicting paradigms. Each paradigm is capable of committing the psychologist to a full-time job reflecting the distinct paradigmatic responsibilities. Hence, the school psychologist attempting to operate within a more holistic paradigm has the arduous task of effectively intervening within the time commitments needed to be responsive in both paradigms.

CONCLUSION

Authors such as Capra (1982) and Kuhn (1970) stipulated that there is a global shift from the mechanistic paradigm to a holistic paradigm. This transformation is a natural transition given the interconnected nature of the earth and its cultures. Nations cannot stop a paradigm shift, they can only adjust with the transformation or risk cultural decline.

Previously, is was suggested that for restructuring and transformation to occur within education and special education, theorists, practitioners, and policy makers must think and conceptualize human development and learning from a broader, more global viewpoint (Wiest & Kreil, 1995). Bronfenbrenner (1979) refers to this level of systemic thinking as the "macrosystem" and suggests that this cultural framework is the underlying structure for other systems. In essence, we are promulgating the collective examination of our educational norms by coming to some consensus about what we culturally posit and believe. We are also conceptualizing that when queried, most people believe in a multilevel, systems approach to life and development. Currently, it makes the most sense as a model. Hence, consensus about a model of development does not appear so disparate. The difficulty has been that few constituents have thought in a focused manner about the underlying paradigmatic beliefs that influence the policies of education.

Change for school psychology entails the examination of such paradigmatic beliefs, developing consensus about such beliefs, and creating new job roles that represent our beliefs. Naturally, this suggests creating a strong educational program geared for policy makers, intense lobbying for better educational laws (particularly in the area of special education), advocating for a strong preventative role, and a formulating a strong collaboration between practitioners and trainers in higher education. A most disconcerting factor, in an era of cutbacks and limited job security, is that the only legally mandated role of the school psychologist is in the area of assessment, the most reductionistic and mechanistic of roles. Many psychologists, while critical of their disproportionate roles in assessment, are simultaneously fearful of giving up such a legal mandate for fear of losing a vocation. We acknowledge this dilemma, and yet we advocate pushing on with reform and the paradigm shift. School psychologists must embrace a clear focus on a holistic, systems approach, and they must continually publicize their invaluable expertise and training in such areas as counseling, consultation, development, family dynamics, prevention, and intervention. Such effort and energy will launch the profession into the twenty-first century with a clearer relationship between job roles and paradigm.

REFERENCES

Abel, R., & Burke, J. (1985). Perceptions of school psychology services from a staff perspective. *Journal of School Psychology, 23,* 121–131.

Anderson, C. (1983). An ecological developmental model for a family orientation in school psychology. *Journal of School Psychology, 21,* 179–189.

Anderson, W. T., Brown, D. T., & Hohenshil, T. H. (1984). Job satisfaction among practicing school psychologists: A national study. *School Psychology Review, 134,* 225–230.

Bardon, J. (1987). Alternative educational delivery approaches: Implications for school psychology. In J. Graden, J. Zins, & M. Curtis (Eds.), *Alternative educational delivery systems: Enhancing instructional options for all students* (pp. 563–571). Washington, DC: National Association of School Psychologists.

Benson, A. J., & Hughes, J. (1985). Perceptions of role definition processes in school psychology: A national survey. *School Psychology Review, 14,* 64–74.

Bobo, M. (1987). *An ethnographic study of unwilling students.* Unpublished Manuscript, Claremont Graduate School, Claremont, CA.

Bronfenbrenner, U. (1979). *The ecology of human development.* Cambridge, MA: Harvard University Press.

Capra, F. (1982). *The turning point.* New York: Bantam Books.

Coles, G. (1987). *The learning mystique: A critical look at learning disabilities.* New York: Fawcett Columbine.

Dowling, E. & Osborne, E. (1985). *The family and the school: A joint systems approach to problems with children.* London: Routledge & Kegan Paul.

DuCharme, C., Earl, J., & Poplin, M. (1989). *The author model: The constructivist view of the writing process.* Unpublished Manuscript. Claremont Graduate School, Claremont, CA.

Erickson, F. (1987). Transformation and school success: The politics and culture of educational achievement. *Anthropology and Education Quarterly, 18,* 335–356.

Fagan, T. (Ed.). (1989). NASP at twenty. *School Psychology Review, 18.*

Fine, M (1991). *Framing dropouts: Notes on the politics of urban public high schools.* Albany, NY: State University of New York Press.

Fuchs, L., & Fuchs, S. (Eds.). (1986). Linking assessment to instructional intervention: An overview. *School Psychology Review, 15,* 318–323.

Glasser, W. (1990). *Quality schools: Managing students without coercion.* New York: Harper & Row.

Gold, M., & Mann, D. W. (1987). *Expelled to a friendlier place: A study of effective alternative schools.* Ann Arbor, MI: University of Michigan Press.

Goodlad, J. (1984). *A place called school.* New York: McGraw-Hill.

Graden, J., Zins, J., & Curtis, M. (1988). *Alternative educational delivery systems: Enhancing instructional options for all students.* Washington, DC: National Association for School Psychologists.

Griffin, R. (1988). *Underachievers in secondary school: Education off the mark.* Hilldale, NJ: Erlbaum Publishers.

Hart, S. (1987). Psychological maltreatment in schooling. *School Psychology Review, 16,* 169–180.

Hart, S. (1989). NASP at thirty: A vision for children. *School Psychology Review, 18,* 221–224.

Heshusius, L. (1982). The heart of the advocacy dilemma: A mechanistic world view. *Exceptional Children, 49,* 6–13.

Heshusius, L. (1986). Paradigm shifts and special: A response to Ulman and Rosenberg. *Exceptional Children, 52,* 461–465.

Heshusius, L. (1989). The Newtonian mechanistic paradigm, special education, and contours of alternatives: An overview. *Journal of Learning Disabilities, 22,* 403–415.

Huberty, T., & Buebner, E. (1988). A national survey of burnout among school psychologists. *Psychology in the Schools, 25,* 54–61.

Hutton, J., Dubes, R., & Muir, S. (1992). Assessment practices of school psychologists: Ten years later. *School Psychology Review, 21,* 271–284.

Institute for Transformation in Education. (1992). *Voices from the inside: A report on schooling from inside the classroom.* Claremont, CA: The Claremont Graduate School.

Kuhn, T. S. (1970). *The structure of scientific revolution.* Chicago: University of Chicago Press.

Learner-centered psychological principles: Guidelines for school redesign and reform. (1992, September). *NASP Communique,* p. 15.

McLaren, P. (1989). *Life in schools: An introduction to critical pedagogy in the foundations of education.* New York: Longman.

Paget, K. (1987). Systemic family assessment: Concepts and strategies for school psychologists. *School Psychology Review, 16,* 429–442.

Paget, K., & Nagle, R. (1986). A conceptual model of preschool assessment. *School Psychology Review, 15,* 154–165.

Pfeiffer, S., & Dean, R. (Eds.). (1988). Mini-series on school psychologists in non-traditional settings. *School Psychology Review, 17.*

Poplin, M. (1987). Self-imposed blindness: The scientific method in education. *Remedial and Special Education, 8,* 31–37.

Poplin, M. (1988a). The reductionistic fallacy in learning disabilities: Replicating the past by reducing the present. *Journal of Learning Disabilities, 21,* 389–400.

Poplin, M. (1988b). Holistic/Constructivistic principles of the teaching/learning process: Implications for the field of learning disabilities. *Journal of Learning Disabilities, 21,* 401–416.

Power, T., & Bartholomew, K. (1987). Family-school relationship patterns: An ecological assessment. *School Psychology Review, 16,* 498–512.

Reynolds, C., Gutkin, T., Elliot, S., & Witt, J. (1984). *School Psychology: Essentials of theory and practice.* New York: John Wiley & Sons.

Rhodes, L., & Dudley-Marling, C. (1988). *Readers and writers with a difference: A holistic approach to teaching learning disabled and remedial students.* Portsmouth, NH: Heinemann.

Russell, P. (1983). *The global brain: Speculations on the evolutionary leap to planetary consciousness.* Los Angeles: J. P. Tarcher.

Shin, M. (1986). Does anyone care what happens after the refer-test-place sequence: The systematic evaluation of special education program effectiveness. *School Psychology Review, 15,* 49–58.

Shor, I. (1980). *Critical teaching and everyday life.* Chicago: University of Chicago Press.

Slavin, R. E., Madden, N. A., Karweit, N. L., Dolan, L., Wasik, B. A., Shaw, A., Mainzer, K. L., & Haxby, B. (1991). Neverstreaming: Prevention and early intervention as an alternative to special education. *Journal of Learning Disabilities, 24,* 373–378.

Stewart, K. (1986). Innovative practice of indirect service delivery: Realities and idealities. *School Psychology Review, 15,* 466–478.

Stone, S., Poplin, M., Johnson. J., & Simpson, O. (1991). *Nontraditional talents of the learning disabled: Divergent thinking and feeling.* Unpublished Manuscript, Claremont Graduate School, Claremont, CA.

Stone, S., Poplin, M., Johnson, J., & Simpson, O. (1992). Nontraditional talents of the learning disabled: Music and art. Unpublished manuscript, The Claremont Graduate School, Claremont, CA.

Weaver, C. (1985). Parallels between new paradigms in science and in reading and literacy theories: An essay review. *Research in Teaching English, 19,* 298–316.

West, F., & Idol, L. (1987). School consultation (part I): An interdisciplinary perspective on theory, models, and research. *Journal of Learning Disabilities, 20.*

Wiest, D. J. (1991, March). *Service delivery in the twenty-first century: The role of the holistic school psychologist.* Paper presented at the California Association of School Psychologists' annual convention, Los Angeles, CA.

Wiest, D. J., & Kreil, D. (1995). Transformational obstacles in special education. *Journal of Learning Disabilities, 28*(7), 399–407.

Wiest, D. J. & Stone, S. (1993). *Holistic approaches in special education: Creating a framework for attention deficit-hyperactivity disorder students.* Unpublished manuscript, The Claremont Graduate School, Claremont, CA.

Zins, J., & Forman, S. (Eds.). (1988). Primary prevention in the schools: What are we waiting for (mini-series)? *School Psychology Review, 17.*

5

Restructuring Classroom Management for More Interactive and Integrated Teaching and Learning

Barbara Larrivee

INTRODUCTION

The movement from more traditional teacher-directed classroom structures to structures in which students are active participants in the teaching-learning process necessitates a reconceptualization of what constitutes effective classroom management practices. While current notions about best management practices may be appropriate for classroom organizations in which instruction is primarily teacher-directed, effectively managing classroom environments in which students are interactive participants in the learning process, rather than passive recipients of teacher-directed instruction, will require a shift away from teacher control–student compliance patterns of interaction. This new role definition for students creates new task demands, placing students in a variety of interactive settings in which the predominant work style is no longer independent but cooperative and collaborative. Engaging students in more active roles as learners will require students to develop autonomy from the teacher. These changing demands of the classroom setting call for a restructuring of classroom management and interaction styles to better align with emerging metaphors of teacher as social mediator and learning facilitator.

The traditional classroom has changed considerably since the emergence in the 1970s and early 1980s of our knowledge base on effective practices for classroom management, pioneered by the work of Kounin (1970) and followed by a host of other researchers (see Brophy, 1983, 1988; Doyle, 1986; Evertson, 1985, 1989; Evertson, Emmer, Clements, & Worsham, 1994; Evertson, Emmer, Sanford, & Clements, 1983; Evertson & Weade, 1989). The changing demands of the classroom setting warrant reexamination of commonly held beliefs about what constitutes effective classroom management practices.

Increasing diversity of the student population is providing the impetus for creating a more responsive educational system to better serve all students, especially those currently at risk of school failure. Teachers continue to face new instructional and management challenges as they attempt to accommodate a wider range of student learning styles and behavior patterns. Serving all at-risk learners primarily in general education classroom settings necessitates a broader conceptualization of classroom management going beyond organizational aspects (e.g., group management, establishing routines, and lesson planning and delivery) and strategies for student compliance (e.g., behavior modification, intervention strategies, and assertive discipline) to include emphasis on developing student autonomy by enhancing students' development of problem-solving skills, adaptive learning strategies, and appropriate social skills as well as effective interpersonal and communication styles.

CHANGING ROLES FOR TEACHERS AND STUDENTS

Not only are the student population and instructional delivery models changing but major curricular changes are challenging traditional student-teacher interaction patterns. The movement toward providing greater emphasis on curricular integration, teaching for meaning, interactive dialogue, socialization, and collaboration will require a restructuring of classroom management and teacher discourse patterns. Our current knowledge base on effective classroom management practices was established during an era in which the model was primarily one of the teacher providing direct instruction and students working independently. Brophy

(1988) characterizes this approach as the "whole-class instruction/recitation/seatwork" approach.

Fundamental changes in the way classrooms function necessitate that educators reconceptualize and restructure classroom organizations and task structures as well as performance expectations. The traditional classroom setting has been characterized by the teacher primarily providing direct instruction, carefully structuring student response patterns, closely monitoring student feedback, and keeping students on task during seatwork activities, largely completed independently. When we instead ask students to be active participants in the teaching-learning process and to function effectively in a variety of collaborative modes with peers, these changes in task demands call for a restructuring of classroom management practices.

Conceptions of effective classroom management need to be reexamined in light of emerging beliefs about quality teaching. The shift in the learning environment from the traditional classroom to a more interactive setting is characterized by a move from teacher-directed lessons to participatory learning, from predetermined learning outcomes to less-defined learning outcomes, from uniform assessment of performance to varied assessment of mastery of concepts, from sequenced curriculum to integrated curriculum, from teacher solicitation of specific student responses to interactive dialogue, and from the teacher questioning students to reciprocal teaching.

The student role is changing from passive recipient of teacher-directed instruction to interactive participant in the teaching-learning process. The teacher role is changing from controlling learning to facilitating learning. This transformation is guided by assumptions about teaching and learning that move us from the belief that students learn from paying attention to the teacher and repetition and rote memory to the belief that students construct their own meaning and have responsibility for their own learning. This view of the teaching-learning process reframes the teacher role from one of concern for the function of learning to one of concern for the facilitation of learning.

Engaging students in more active roles as learners and increasingly calling on students to make choices in terms of both academic tasks as well as behavior will also call for a shift in emphasis from teacher control to student self-management. Teacher belief systems about power and control will require reexamination as teachers are challenged to create collaborative climates in which both teachers and students have shared responsibility for establishing an optimal climate for learning.

EMERGING BELIEFS ABOUT QUALITY TEACHING

Historically, conceptions of good teaching have evolved from primarily good discipline in the 1960s, to efficient and careful monitoring of student work in the 1970s, to increasing levels of student on task engagement in the 1980s, to emphasis on how learning occurs and development of lifelong learners in the 1990s. The trend represents a gradual relinquishing of control for learning from teachers to students. However, there has not been a corresponding shift in emphasis relative to classroom management and student-teacher interaction styles to accompany the academic shift from teacher control to development of greater student autonomy (e.g., Bullough, 1994; Marshall, 1992; Randolph & Evertson, 1994).

Currently, a misalignment exists between an advocated curriculum that seeks to promote problem solving and create meaningful learning experiences and an authoritative stance for managing classrooms. As McCaslin and Good (1992) have pointed out, "discordant messages about students are mirrored in current patterns of classroom management that are antithetical to present curriculum reform and professed educational goals" (p. 8). A curriculum designed to produce self-motivated, active learners is undermined by classroom management practices that encourage, if not demand, blind obedience. The enhancement of self-motivation and participatory learning is not accomplished by the production of obedient workers. Moreover, if we persist in preparing students for nonexistent "factory work," we will fail to prepare them for the complex and interdependent world they live in.

Although the basic skills approach and the teaching of isolated subject matter has served us well in past generations, it will not prepare students to survive in the future or to take their place in a global society. Technological advances are occurring at such a rate and our scientific notions are in such a state of flux that a firm statement made today will almost certainly be modified by the time the student gets around to using the knowledge. Hence, we are faced with an entirely new situation in education where the goal of education is no longer the maintenance of the status quo but, rather, the promotion of change. Education should create a mindfulness allowing individuals to perceive the universal network of interdependence in which our actions are imbedded.

As Mihaly Csikszentmihalyi notes, in *The Evolving Self: A Psychology for the Third Millennium* (1993), we typically teach each academic subject as if it has an existence independent from others, failing to develop an awareness of integrativeness and interdependence. History can be truly understood only within the framework of the coexisting economic, social, and psychological climate in which human action takes place. For example, we teach children conservation in physics—that each action produces an equal and opposite reaction—as if it were a law that applied only to pistons in an engine, while failing to develop an awareness that the principle applies equally to human psychology, to social action, to economics, in fact, to the entire planetary system.

Classroom management should do more than ensure compliance; it should enhance self-understanding and self-reflection and promote self-management and self-discipline. Rogers and Freiberg (1994) advocate for "people-centered" classrooms in which a "cooperative social fabric" is created, embodied in self-discipline. They use "self-discipline" as an all-inclusive term, encompassing making choices, setting goals, helping and caring for others, listening, establishing trust, and engaging in self-reflection.

INCOMPATIBILITY OF THE BEHAVIORAL PARADIGM WITH EMERGING BELIEFS ABOUT QUALITY TEACHING

Traditionally, effective classroom management has been largely viewed as tantamount to controlling student behavior, keeping students on task, and maintaining lesson flow, calling for constant teacher vigilance and appropriate teacher intervention. Furthermore, student behavior is judged to be inappropriate irrespective of consideration of individual student characteristics, performance expectations, or appropriateness of the learning task. The implicit assumption is that students are unable or unwilling to exercise control and/or solve their problems. Hence teachers impose their

requirements for order without relating them to student requirements for learning.

Thus the concept of control is equated with the teacher's perception of the student's ability to behave appropriately or solve problems. Teachers' belief systems about their primary role with respect
to classroom management influence their behavior-control styles
and their use of power and control (Larrivee, 1995). When teachers
believe students choose not to provide an appropriate solution,
they impose a solution. When teachers believe students are not
capable of providing a solution, then they may provide an adapta-
tion, either in task structure or performance expectation. Although
teacher perception of student needs relative to classroom control
are viewed quite differently in these two approaches (i.e., in the first
case teachers see students as needing to be disciplined, whereas in
the second case they see students as needing to be helped), in both
cases the teacher takes responsibility, either by exercising control
or by applying structure. Although the latter approach may be
more humane, both of these approaches socialize students to expect to have problems solved for them. These views relative to
classroom management may be appropriate for classroom organizations in which instruction is primarily teacher-directed and
where the teacher is the primary decision maker; however, these
approaches do not hold students responsible and thus are not likely
to build student competence and/or autonomy for eventual self-
management.

Teachers are generally placed in the role of managing student
behavior in order to maintain an environment conducive to teaching and learning. When attempting to change or deal with students'
inappropriate behavior, the typical teacher response is to try to
control deviant behavior by exercising power and control, rather
than consider the appropriateness of the learning context for accommodating individual student needs. Teachers can choose to
manage student behavior by using their authority and exercising
direct control by dispensing rewards and punishment, or they can
choose not to use their power in favor of strategies that empower
students to make their own choices.

Traditional wisdom for managing individual student behavior
and maintaining order in the classroom has relied on the use of
extrinsic rewards and punishment, praise, modeling, and teacher

evaluation of appropriate behavior and acceptable work. When teachers use consequences to manage students' behavior, they are using their authority position to convince students to control their behavior. Basically, teachers either reward students for behaving appropriately or punish them for behaving inappropriately. Research has clearly demonstrated that individuals respond better to positive reinforcement than they do to punishment; thus the emphasis for school-based behavior and classroom management has been on identifying and dispensing rewards that will develop, sustain, or increase behaviors that are deemed appropriate for the classroom setting.

Relying primarily on the behavioral model for classroom management does have certain benefits. The foremost is that it offers teachers positive alternatives for working with students and helps them refrain from using reprimands and punishment to control student behavior. Also, the behavioral approach, with its emphasis on rewarding appropriate behavior, helps teachers focus on identifying potentially meaningful reinforcers for students; it is therefore more likely to produce positive and supportive interactions with students. Its focus on actual behaviors also helps teachers to be more objective and refrain from labeling students' character (e.g., lazy, inconsiderate, or manipulative).

Although the behavioral approach does, for the most part, get students to comply with the teacher's demands, it does not enhance student autonomy; rather, it perpetuates student reliance on the teacher. Several issues raised by researchers serve to question the use of rewards and punishment to modify student behavior.

Although the behavioral approach has several benefits, it is not without its potential drawbacks. Some research findings, especially relative to the effects of contingent use of rewards on classroom behavior, indicate that the relationship between rewards and punishment and subsequent individual student behavior is more complex than had been assumed by those advocating primary use of the behavioral approach for managing classroom behavior. Several issues have been raised by researchers that serve to question the use of rewards and punishment to modify student behavior. One issue relates to the alignment of teacher intention with actual student effect. Students don't always experience consequences congruent with the teacher's intention. For example, praising certain students in front of their peers can be counterproductive. For some students, teacher attention in the form of recognition or praise is embarrassing or threatening rather than rewarding. Extrinsic positive reinforcement doesn't always increase desired behavior. Under certain conditions, positive reinforcement can have detrimental effects. Using rewards for desired behavior and academic performance can erode intrinsic motivation (Doyle, 1986; Lapper, 1983). Students who are already motivated to learn can lose their intrinsic motivation to do so if they become too interested in earning extrinsic rewards (e.g., Centra & Chambers, 1978; DeCharms, 1976; Deci, 1976, 1978; Lapper & Greene, 1978; Pittman, Boggiano, & Ruble, 1982; Ross, 1976).

Furthermore, the behavioral change brought about by positive and negative reinforcements in one situation has not been shown to generalize to other situations (e.g., classes, teachers, or environments) or to be maintained when the extrinsic reinforcers are dropped (Brophy & Putnam, 1978; Emery & Marholin, 1977). In addition, the effectiveness of positive and negative reinforcements as a classroom management tool varies according to the student's age and developmental level, with the pattern being that it is most effective with younger students, somewhat less effective with upper-elementary and middle school students, and least effective with secondary school students (Brophy & Putnam, 1978; Forness, 1973; Stallings, 1975).

Another important issue is that positive reinforcement can increase students' learned helplessness and dependency if they come to rely excessively on teacher approval in lieu of their own motivation (Ginott, 1972; Weiner, 1979). Similarly, positive reinforcement can discourage creativity if students become more concerned about pleasing their teachers or conforming to their teachers' expectations than on finding their own solutions to problems (Johnson & Johnson, 1975; Soar & Soar, 1975).

Inhibiting behavior should not be confused with instilling attitudes—student obedience cannot be equated with student motivation. Conditions that foster quick obedience do not foster internalization of self-control, and internalized self-control, or self-regulation, is necessary to function adaptively both in classrooms and in society (e.g., Kohn, 1993; Lapper, 1983; McCaslin & Good, 1992). As long as conceptions of classroom management remain rooted in the behavioral paradigm of teaching, the responsibility for student motivation and effort will fall largely on teachers and outside of students themselves.

Another potential danger with the use of consequences to control students not often considered is that it can serve to insulate teachers from important feedback on their classroom practices. For example, students might disguise the fact that they are bored, frustrated, or even angry because of feared negative consequences. Hence, teachers fail to realize the need to use other strategies that might enhance learning and student-teacher relationships. Such lack of feedback can also serve to sustain inferior or less-effective teaching practices (Grossman, 1990; Ryan, 1979).

Effective classroom management is inextricably tied to the quality of educational experiences in which students engage as well as the teacher's skill in organizing the class structure to facilitate efficient teaching and learning. Successful teachers actually avoid many potential behavior problems by using effective teaching techniques, appropriately challenging students, promoting group accountability and cohesiveness, preventing potentially disruptive situations from occurring, establishing reasonable procedures and rules, modeling desirable behavior, satisfying students' basic needs, and maintaining good relationships with students. For many students who behave inappropriately in spite of their teachers' best efforts at preventive planning, eliminating situational or contextual barriers, teaching them coping skills or reasoning with them will often be all that is needed. Still, some students, especially younger students still in the early stages of moral development and older students who are testing the waters, will need to be shown that it is to their advantage to behave appropriately by applying appropriate consequences.

Extrinsic reinforcers are sometimes the only way to get some students to behave appropriately, especially those who have a history of unsuccessful school experiences and very limited success with classroom learning tasks. Even for these students, however, once more adaptive behavior is demonstrated, other strategies that help them develop their own self-control should be introduced. It may also be necessary to use consequences to suppress, control, and redirect behavior that is aggressive, abusive, or disruptive to learning. For this reason, it is important for teachers to have such strategies in their repertoire. However, teachers should view getting students to behave in a desired way for the moment with extrinsic motivation as only a short-term goal. Motivating students to want to behave appropriately is the ultimate long-range goal and involves systematically supporting students' independence and self-management. Teachers who are most successful in dealing with students who pose behavior challenges use long-term, solution-oriented approaches rather than short-term desist-and-control responses (Brophy & McCaslin, 1992). In so doing, they typically enlist students to become active participants in developing a resolution to the problem.

THE PERILS OF PRAISE AS A MANAGEMENT TOOL

Promoting student autonomy involves supporting students in self-evaluation, self-analysis, and self-reflection so that they will learn self-management and self-control. With this end in mind, the traditional wisdom of teacher praise can also be challenged on the grounds that praise conditions students to seek outside evaluation for accomplishments rather than develop responsibility for their own behavior (Larrivee, 1992). Although praise can have positive effects on student behavior, substantial evidence shows that the use of praise can also have undesirable effects. Furthermore, effective use of praise is related not to quantity or the frequency of praise but, rather, to the qualitative use of praise, considering when and how to use praise. As students get older they become less extrinsically motivated and more intrinsically motivated. Hence effective praise is matched to students' developmental levels. This calls for teachers to move away from strictly evaluative praise and move toward encouraging personal satisfaction, self-reflection, and analysis by calling on students to assess their performance by their own standards, feelings, and sense of accomplishment.

Depending on a student's prior experience with feedback and the way it is delivered, praise may serve as a reinforcer, as a punisher, or as a powerless antecedent that has no effect on either the alteration of inappropriate behavior or the continuation of desired behavior. In his review of the research on teacher praise, Brophy (1981) concluded that indiscriminate praise or mere frequency of praise is not positively related to student learning.

However, providing feedback as to the correctness of student responses with moderate levels of praise issued for quality responses is positively related to student learning. Praise should reward effort as well as success and should be given because students deserve it, not because they seek it. Brophy also questioned the practice of praising low-achieving students for putting forth minimal effort, noting that praise given to low-achieving students for trivial accomplishments can actually worsen not improve students' functioning. Students may doubt their own ability or lose confidence if they feel they are being praised for insignificant accomplishments. Similarly, the praise or reward may seem insincere, irrelevant, or not credible if given for every minimal act performed.

Rudolph Dreikurs clearly distinguishes between praise and encouragement and makes a strong case against the use of praise, favoring instead the language of encouragement (Dreikurs, Grunwald, & Pepper, 1982). Praise positively evaluates students' performance; on the other hand, encouragement conveys teacher respect and belief in students' capabilities. Through encouragement teachers give purpose to learning and facilitate the development of a positive self-image. When teachers construe ability as an acquirable skill, deemphasizing competitive social comparison while emphasizing self-comparison of progress and personal accomplishments, they help students build a sense of self-efficacy that promotes academic achievement (Bandura, 1993).

Praise conditions students to seek outside evaluation for their accomplishments and perpetuates the attitude "What am I going to get out of this?" Encouragement recognizes efforts, not necessarily achievements, and stimulates motivation from within, allowing students to become aware of their own strengths. Whereas praise conditions students to measure their worth by their ability to please others, encouragement teaches students to evaluate their own progress and make their own decisions.

Haim Ginott (1972) similarly warns of the drawbacks of using praise, especially when it is judgmental. As with negative comments, praise can have detrimental effects on forming a positive self-image. When teachers use praise to tell students they are good because they know the right answer, students logically conclude that they are bad when they do not know the answer. Such equating of knowledge with goodness is dangerous. It's important not to equate "knowing the right answer" with "being good." For correct answers, teachers should use comments that carry no evaluation of the student's character; they might say, for example, "Fine," "Exactly," "That's correct," or "You're right."

Evaluative praise is often an attempt by the teacher to ensure desired behavior. When students feel that the praise is not sincere but delivered to manipulate them into behaving in a certain way, they can harbor resentment. As an alternative to providing evaluative praise, teachers can comment on student efforts, describe their own feelings, or provide honest recognitions without value judgments. Nonevaluative statements communicate appreciation and acceptance while allowing students to make their own evaluations about their behavior and work.

Thomas Gordon (1974) also makes several assertions about praise. Teachers almost universally resist the notion that praise could serve as a roadblock or nonfacilitative response when responding to messages that indicate a student is experiencing a problem. After all, teachers have been trained to reinforce "good behavior," as determined by the teacher, by systematically dispensing rewards, and among these are praise, positive evaluation, or kind words of support. However, a student experiencing a problem often feels personal dissatisfaction. Praise when the student is in this state either goes "unheard," makes the student feel that the teacher does not really understand, or provokes an even stronger defense of the student's low evaluation of himself or herself. A positive evaluation that does not fit with the student's self-image may invoke anger for the student may perceive it as an attempt at manipulation. Furthermore, in the classroom setting, praise given to one student, or to a few, will often be translated by the other students as negative evaluation of them. Similarly, a student who has become accustomed to receiving frequent evaluative praise may feel negatively evaluated when he or she does not get praised. Students grow to depend on praise—even to demand it.

FOSTERING STUDENT AUTONOMY

Moving away from the primary role of providing rewards and punishments, delivering praise, directing classroom activities, evaluating student performance, and judging student behavior calls for a significant shift. Changing the metaphor of teacher from manager, organizer, and boss to monitor, facilitator, and leader represents a major transformation. In order to transform the traditional classroom into a learning community, students need to feel secure, in terms not only of physical safety but psychological security as well. Students need to feel free to express themselves, to feel valued as group members, and to be accepted as individuals. By the dialogue they create with students teachers play a critical role in modeling freedom of expression and acceptance. Developing a safe environment calls for attending to students' emotional and personal needs concurrently with their academic and social needs. In such a teaching and learning climate, emphasis is placed on the quality of human interactions, both between teacher and student and between student and student.

Several authors who have translated their principles of human interactions into strategies for classroom teachers offer alternative models to compliance models for creating an optimal atmosphere for teaching and learning. Thomas Gordon's (1974) work on recognizing roadblocks to communication provides strategies for building effective communication channels and establishing supportive relationships with students. The work of William Glasser, from the 1960s through the 1990s, emphasizes the importance of satisfying students' basic needs as a necessary condition to establish a learning community. These basic human needs include the need to belong, the need to have power and freedom, and the need to experience personal satisfaction. Understanding the motivation that drives students' behavior based on the work of Dreikurs and colleagues (1968, 1972, 1982) offers still another perspective. Dreikurs reminds us that we all need to have avenues for receiving recognition. If the classroom environment fails to offer students opportunities to get recognition, students will find ways, often inappropriate, to get the recognition they crave. Enhancing student self-esteem through continuous encouragement and validating and accepting both teachers' and students' feelings is the means for developing a positive socioemotional climate advocated by Haim Ginott (1972).

From the work of these authors several themes relative to classroom interactions emerge. These consistent themes call for minimizing blame by clearly differentiating between rejection of the student's behavior and rejection of the student, allowing and encouraging student choices, and providing continuous encouragement while, at the same time, calling on students to take responsibility for their own behavior. However, because students have typically been socialized to a classroom environment in which the teacher directs activities, manages student behavior, and evaluates student performance, asking students to be responsible for their own behavior will require a major restructuring. Teachers can facilitate this shift by asking students to engage in self-evaluation, not only of the appropriateness of their behavior but of the quality of their classroom performance. The notion of self-evaluation is a key concept for establishing shared responsibility for maintaining a supportive learning climate.

FOSTERING STUDENT SELF-EVALUATION AND SELF-REFLECTION

Fostering student self-evaluation will require that teachers restructure their discourse patterns and pay particular attention to the language they use when giving feedback to students. Most responses to others in general, but especially to students, are judgmental. Certainly teachers must at times exercise control and serve in an evaluative and judgmental role, but there are many instances in which teachers can allow students to make their own judgments about the appropriateness of their behavior and the quality of their work. The process of evaluating and judging students inhibits acceptance. Nonjudgmental responses facilitate the development of responsible behavior by granting students the responsibility for their behavior. Because evaluative responses are so ingrained, making the change from giving evaluative feedback to students will take a sustained effort to monitor responses to students.

Transforming from evaluative to nonevaluative responses will require a restructuring of classroom discourse. One alternative to using evaluative language when responding to student behavior is to provide a simple description of the student's behavior, ensuring that the words chosen are not value-laden. For example, the teacher might say, "This is the second time this week you've been late" as opposed to "You're being irresponsible." Clearly, the first response is far more likely to solicit a dialogue in which the student takes responsibility for his or her behavior.

Another way to avoid evaluative language is to identify with the feeling underlying the behavior and respond in a manner that conveys understanding and acceptance of the feeling, not necessarily agreement, while neither encouraging nor discouraging the feeling. Acknowledging the feeling keeps the responsibility with the student and helps the student solve the problem but still maintains the teacher's involvement. Making a statement like "I see you're upset about what happened in math class" neither condones nor criticizes the student's behavior; instead it acknowledges the emotional state that underlies the behavior. If necessary, the follow-up to this statement could take the form of a solicitation of what the student needs, as in "Do you need to take a minute to pull yourself together?" Responding to students with acceptance is preferable to judgmental responses, whether they be judgmental-positive or judgmental-negative, because such responses recognize that each individual is ultimately responsible for himself or herself. The notion of acceptance versus judgment is closely aligned with Glasser's (1985) notion of control theory in which he posits that while we may try to control others' behavior, in actuality we can control only our own behavior. When we evaluate another's behavior, even with a positive evaluation, we implicitly reserve the right to make a negative evaluation. Either case is an attempt to control the other person by judging that person by some set of standards external to the person.

Glasser (1992) offers another alternative to judgmental responses to students; he advocates that teachers call on students to make value judgments about their own behavior. Comments such as "Is that helping the group?" or "What might you do that would be more helpful?" call on students to take responsibility for their behavior and recognize its effect on self as well as others. Glasser challenges teachers to teach students that freedom is tied to responsibility by attempting to motivate students from within, to help students establish inner controls and learn to regulate their own behavior.

When commenting on written work, teachers can avoid judgmental responses by sharing personal reactions (e.g., "I'm really excited about this idea") or posing questions that extend the student's thinking (e.g., "How has this awareness affected you?"). They can also make specific comments acknowledging progress (e.g., "You've become much clearer in organizing your points") or state a need for greater clarity (e.g., "I'm not sure what you mean here. Can you make this clearer?"). Such constructive comments support students' efforts and build self-confidence while allowing students to draw their own conclusions about their work. Encouraging student self-evaluation by interacting with students in a nonjudmental fashion supports student development of self-management strategies and avoids the drawbacks associated with dispensing rewards and punishment, delivering praise, judging student behavior, and evaluating student performance.

If teachers want to move away from a teacher-controlled environment and call on students to be active participants in making choices and solving problems, they may at least initially have to engage in strategy building to teach students the strategies they may be lacking in areas such as decision making, problem solving, self-control, and conflict resolution. If students are lacking the necessary repertoire to make appropriate choices, then it is incumbent on teachers to teach students strategies so that they will eventually become more capable of making better choices in the future. Thus the teacher may need to provide sequenced lessons and structured experiences to teach students strategies so that in time the teacher can relinquish responsibility to students and function in a more facilitative role where students are expected to make choices, find solutions, and in fact have a response repertoire for making appropriate choices.

Often students fail to act in appropriate ways not because of lack of motivation, conscious choice, or unwillingness but because they have not learned what constitutes acceptable ways of behaving or under what circumstances a behavior would be appropriate or inappropriate. Specific strategy instruction and structured learning experiences can enable students to learn social and self-management skills that will help them develop positive peer relationships, work cooperatively in learning groups, and participate productively in classroom activities. Crucial to this learning is the modeling provided by the teacher, particularly in establishing classroom discourse patterns that manifest the language of acceptance and encouragement.

CONCLUSION

As long as the teacher controls the management system, students will not learn self-management. Students receive competing messages when we teach for meaning and interconnectedness and manage for mere convenience and compliance.

When classrooms embody a spirit of acceptance, mutual tolerance and respect, the consciousness of students and teachers alike is raised to new heights. Such an environment is the foundation for building a caring community and creating lifelong learners.

REFERENCES

Bandura, A. (1993). Perceived self-efficacy in cognitive development and functioning. *Educational Psychologist, 28*(2), 117–148.

Brophy, J. (1981). Teacher praise: A functional analysis. *Review of Educational Research, 51,* 5–32.

Brophy, J. (1983). Classroom organization and management. *Elementary School Journal, 83,* 265–285.

Brophy, J. (1988). Educating teachers about managing classrooms and students. *Teaching and Teacher Education, 4*(1), 1–18.

Brophy, J., & McCaslin, M. (1992). Teachers' reports of how they perceive and cope with problem students. *Elementary School Journal, 93,* 3–68.

Brophy, J. E., & Putnam, J. C. (1978). "Classroom management in the elementary grades." ERIC ED 167, 537.

Bullough, R. V. , Jr. (1994). Digging at the roots: Discipline, management, and metaphor. *Action in Teacher Education 16*(1), 1–10.

Csikszentmihalyi, M. (1993). *The evolving self: A psychology for the third millennium.* New York: HarperCollins.

Condry, J., & Chambers, J. (1978). Intrinsic motivation and the process of learning. In M. R. Lepper & D. Greene (Eds.), *The hidden cost of reward: New perspectives on the psychology of human motivation.* Hillsdale, NJ: Erlbaum.

DeCharms, R. (1976). *Enhancing motivation: Change in the classroom.* New York: Irvington.

Deci, E. L. (1976). *Intrinsic motivation.* New York: Plenum Press.

Deci, E. L. (1978). Applications of research on the effects of rewards. In M. R. Lepper & D. Greene (Eds.), *The hidden costs of reward: New perspectives on the psychology of human motivation.* Hillsdale, NJ: Erlbaum.

Doyle, W. (1986). Classroom organization and management. In M. C. Wittrock (Ed.), *Handbook of Research on Teaching* (3rd ed., pp. 392–431). New York: Macmillan.

Dreikurs, R. (1968). *Psychology in the classroom: A manual for teachers* (2nd ed.). New York: Harper & Row.

Dreikurs, R., & Cassel, P. (1972). *Discipline without tears.* New York: Hawthorn.

Dreikurs, R., Grunwald, B., & Pepper, F. (1982). *Maintaining sanity in the classroom.* New York: Harper & Row.

Emery, R., & Marholin, D. (1977). An applied behavior analysis of delinquency: The irrelevancy of relevant behavior. *American Psychologist, 32,* 860–873.

Evertson, C. M. (1985). Training teachers in classroom management: An experimental study in secondary school classrooms. *Journal of Educational Research, 79,* 51–58.

Evertson, C. M. (1989). Improving elementary classroom management: A school-based training program for beginning the year. *Journal of Educational Research, 83,* 82–90.

Evertson, C. M., Emmer, E., Clements, B., & Worsham, M. (1994). *Classroom management for elementary teachers* (3rd ed.). Boston: Allyn & Bacon.

Evertson, C. M., Emmer, E., Sanford, J., & Clements, B. (1983). Improving classroom management: An experiment in elementary classrooms. *Elementary School Journal, 84,* 173–188.

Evertson, C. M., & Weade, R. (1989). Classroom management and teaching style: Instructional stability and variability in two junior high English classrooms. *Elementary School Journal, 89*(3), 379–393.

Forness, S. R. (1973). The reinforcement hierarchy. *Psychology in the Schools, 10,* 168–177.

Ginott, H. (1972). *Teacher and child.* New York: Avon.

Glasser, W. (1985). *Control theory in the classroom.* New York: Perennial Library.

Glasser, W. (1992). *The quality school: Managing students without coercion.* New York: Harper & Row.

Gordon, T. (1974). *T.E.T. Teacher effectiveness training.* New York: David McKay.

Grossman, H. (1990). *Trouble-free teaching: Solutions to behavior problems in the classroom.* Mountain View, CA: Mayfield.

Johnson, D., & Johnson, R. (1975). *Learning together and alone: Cooperation, competition, and individualization.* Englewood Cliffs, NJ: Prentice-Hall.

Kohn, A. (1993). *Punished by rewards.* Boston: Houghton Mifflin.

Kounin, J. (1970). *Discipline and group management in classrooms.* New York: Holt, Rinehart & Winston.

Larrivee, B. (1992). *Strategies for effective classroom management: Creating a collaborative climate.* Boston: Allyn & Bacon.

Lepper, M. (1983). Extrinsic reward and intrinsic motivation: Implications for the classroom. In J. Levine & M. Wang (Eds.), *Teacher-student perceptions: Implications for learning.* Hillsdale, NJ: Erlbaum.

Lepper, M., & Greene, D. (Eds.). (1978). *The hidden costs of reward: New perspectives on the psychology of human motivation.* Hillsdale, NJ: Erlbaum.

Marshall, H. H. (Ed.). (1992). *Redefining student learning: Roots of educational change.* Norwood, NJ: Ablex.

McCaslin, M., & Good, T. L. (1992). Compliant cognition: The misalliance of management and instructional goals in current school reform. *Educational Researcher, 21*(3), 4–17.

Pittman, T., Boggiano, A., & Ruble, D. (1982). Intrinsic and extrinsic motivational orientations: Limiting conditions on the undermining and enhancing effects of reward on intrinsic motivation. In J. Levine & M. Wang (Eds.), *Teacher-student perceptions: Implications for learning.* Hillsdale, NJ: Erlbaum.

Randolph, C. H., & Evertson, C. M. (1994). Images of management for learner-centered classrooms. *Action in Teacher Education, 16*(1), 55–63.

Rogers, C., & Freiberg, H. J. (1994). *Freedom to learn* (3rd ed.). New York: Merrill.

Ross, M. (1976). The self-perception of intrinsic motivation. In J. H. Harvey, W. J. Ickes, & R. F. Kidd (Eds.), *New directions in attributional research* (Vol. 1). Hillsdale, NJ: Erlbaum.

Ryan, B. (1979). A case against behavior modification in the "ordinary classroom." *Journal of School Psychology, 17*(2), 131–136.

Soar, R., & Soar, R. (1975). Classroom behavior, pupil characteristics, and pupil growth for the school year and summer. *JSAS Catalog of Selected Documents in Psychology, 5,* 873.

Stallings, J. (1975). Implementation and child effects of teaching practices in Follow Through classrooms. *Monographs of the Society for Research in Child Development, 40,* 7–8.

Weiner, B. (1979). A theory of motivation in some classroom experiences. *Journal of Educational Psychology, 71,* 3–25.

6

From Alienating to Liberating Experiences: A New Comer's Learning Experiences in the New Culture

Danling Fu

Seven years ago, after I taught English for seven years at a college in China, I came to America to pursue a graduate degree. Before I left for America, many friends and colleagues who had been studying abroad warned me, "If you can, try not to major in English. It seems they don't read the same way as we do. You could never get it. It is their literature, we have no say about it." At that time, I did not understand what they meant, and I could not see giving up studying the Western literature I had loved since my childhood. Besides, what they said made me curious about the difference between the Westerner's and Chinese ways of reading.

Before I started school, I listened to, and later read by myself, many Western fairy tales and children's literature like *Cinderella*, *Little Red Riding Hood*, *Frog Prince*, *The Match Girl*, *The Ugly Duckling*, etc. I was fascinated by the Western world, its culture, its ways of living, its customs, and its ways of thinking and ways with words. Since those stories opened my mind to that far-away land, I became interested in anything about that Western world. I wanted to know about that world more and more. I never stopped reading, dreaming and imagining about the people and life there.

When all schools closed during the Cultural Revolution (1966–1976) in China, I was sent to work on a farm during my teens. I secretly sneaked into the attic, where a dozen trunks full of books were stored. The trunks had been sealed to "prevent from poisoning the people with the Western bourgeoisie ideology." I packed my suitcases with those "poisonous" books, and left for the farm.

For four years on the farm, under the dim kerosene lamp, I educated myself with those books. They were translations of literature from Russia, Germany, France, Britain, Spain, etc. I read every night after working in the field or on rainy or snowy days when I did not have to work. From those readings, I learned the European history, geography, many different countries and cultures. In those books, my mind traveled all over the world. At that time, I lived with four other girls of my age. I shared my reading with them while working in the field or resting in our straw-roofed mud shed. They became more and more interested in my books and started to read on their own. We talked about our reading, and dreamed and imagined together what it would be like to live in the world we read about. Our little shed became a book club. Even many peasants came to listen to our stories. Once a peasant said to me, "Danling, if you die today, you won't regret, as you have known so much about the world." His words made me feel rich. The reading made those years of hard life more tolerable, enjoyable and meaningful. Now looking back at those years, I realize that was the time I read and enjoyed the reading more than any time in my life.

Years later when I had a chance to go to college, I majored in English. I was so thrilled when the first time I was able to read the original version of a book in English instead of the translation. From that time on I immersed myself in English and American literature. From Chaucer, Milton, and Shakespeare to Hawthorne, Melville, Dickenson, Hemingway, Steinbeck, and Mark Twain I learned the development of the British and American culture, language, history and people. The learning of that world and its language inflamed my desire to see that world, experience that culture and know the people there. I dreamed some day I would read that world together with the people there.

In 1985, my life-long dream came true when I was offered an opportunity to study in America. How could I understand and accept the advice from many friends and colleagues that suggested

I give up something I had loved for my whole life? I still vividly remember what they said to me:

It [the Western literature] is something you can never get. It is their literature and culture. It is in their blood and you can never understand or learn to read their works in their way. It is okay to study it here because we use our ways to interpret and understand it. Literature is the most difficult subject for the people like us to learn in America as we didn't grow up there. Don't try to get any degrees in the field of literature in America. It will kill you no matter how hard you try. Just imagine any foreigners would understand our classics like *The Dreams of the Red Chamber* as we do. It is impossible for them, just like the study of their literature is impossible for us. That is why you can hardly see any Oriental faces in the liberal arts field, even few American Chinese there. The Westerners read differently from us, we can never get it. Majoring in anything for us is easier than literature in America.

Their words were very persuasive, but taking their advice was out of the question for me at that time. The literature had given me the most joy and meaning in my life so far. I had wanted to learn how the Western people interpreted their world and words through their literature. I wanted to find out the difference between my way of interpreting their world and theirs. I wanted to be able to enjoy their literature with the depth as I did with my Chinese literature. I wanted to learn more about that culture and world, which was introduced to me through literature since I was a child. When I was reading foreign literature, there were always some hints, some nuance, some implications or words between the lines that I would miss. I wanted to study with the literature in its native land so the people there would help me to understand things that I had no way to learn in China.

As soon as I arrived in America, without any hesitation, I applied to study in an English master program in a college. Before I started my English courses, my mind was filled with joy and excitement when I pictured myself sitting among all Americans discussing the literature, their world and culture. I thought that I was going to get the most "authentic" interpretation of American literature!

Every time before I went to a class, I would carefully read the assignment, twice at least. But when the discussion began, it was as if I was reading a different book from anyone else in the class. I expected we would discuss our interpretations of the text, how the author tried to tell us about his or her world and time, and how the writing reflected his or her ways of understanding the world and the time. But almost in every literature course, the discussion would focus more on the art of composing rather than the meaning of a text, such as symbolism, Romanticism, imagery, literature elements, structure of a text, or the language and the tone of a text. Characters were not analyzed as people, and a setting was not looked at as a place. But they were simply elements of a text structure. A text was discussed as if it had nothing to do with the real world and people. With this way of reading the text, it seemed that the author did not mean to write to express himself or herself or intend to tell the readers something through the writing, but only to show how he or she could manipulate words and language. I could not understand why the art of composing was so over stressed at the expense of the meaning of the text. How could I be interested in the structure of a text before it made enough sense to me?

I became more and more lost and confused in classes. It seemed I was too far behind my peers. I had many questions that concerned the meaning of the text, and wished the class discussion would help me solve those problems. But the class always jumped into the discussion of some kind of "*ism*" at the very first minute. Then I became too confused or overwhelmed to ask, or even remember any of my questions. Very often I left the class, feeling humiliated and frustrated. I did not think I knew everything or could even read. Once I told one of my classmates about my frustration and asked how I could learn to read like they did. He took me to the library, pointing at the reference books and said to me, "Those books will help you, especially those *Cliff Notes.*"

The reference books and *Cliff Notes* were saviors. I spent more time reading them than the assignment itself before I went to class. I learned to rely heavily on them for every writing assignment. I tried to imitate the right "tone" and adopt "the Western ways" of reading. The more I became dependent on the reference books and critics' work for my reading and writing, the more I felt I could not read and write. I did not think I had any background to study the Western literature and blamed my Chinese professors for not teaching me this way to read and write in China.

However, no matter how hard I tried to learn the "proper" ways to read and write about literature, I continued to suffer the loss and confusion. Once we read a poem, which ended with some lines about waves splashing on the rocks on the shore. I liked this image a lot. To me, it portrayed the power and the beauty of nature: when shapeless and colorless waves formed together moving toward the same destination, they created shape, color, strength and noise. They symbolized solidarity and determination. But when I went to the class, I was shocked by how some of my American peers looked at this image. They saw it as a typical sexual image: hard rock surrounded by foams created by striking of waves on the rock. I became speechless by the world of difference between the way my peers and I interpreted this image. When I found no one reacted like I did and all the class including the professor agreeably joined the discussion, I felt so left out. I never thought "literature" would be a world so unfamiliar, remote and strange to me, I wondered "Do all Americans read and talk about literature like this?"

I became more and more silent and felt more and more alienated in classes as the semesters went by. I stopped thinking, or even trying to understand the others. I lost interest in reading and was burdened by all the writing assignments. I developed a knot in my stomach every time on the way to class. I wished I would have taken my friends' advice and not gotten myself into this mess and confusion. Being a successful student in China, I used to like challenge in my learning, but at that time, I felt so helpless, incapable and defeated, as if I were lost in a strange jungle.

I expected the study of American literature would help me not only understand the English language better, but more importantly, understand the American people, culture and world. For instance, when I read *The Adventures of Huckleberry Finn*, I wanted to learn in what way the character Finn represented American youngsters at the time, what American values Mark Twain conveyed through the characterization of Finn, how American people identified themselves with Finn and any other characters in the story, and how Black Americans interpreted Twain's ways of the characterization of Jim. But when we studied this book in class, the discussion was either on the possible homosexual relationship between Finn and Jim, or on black dialect used in the writing. The discussion, which connected so little with the real world and people, did not help me understand the story much, but left me with more blankness about this world, and remoteness toward its people.

I took many courses and studied various literature genres in the English program. There were dramas, poetry, novels and short stories. But I could hardly remember what I read, and even forgot most of the titles and authors. Strangely I can still remember very well the books I read when I was a child or on the farm twenty or thirty years ago. When I talk about those books I still have the intimate feelings and joy associated with those readings. I even can recite some of the lines and quotations from what I read years ago.

When I received my master's degree upon the graduation, instead of feeling a sense of accomplishment or pride, felt relieved, and disabled. But I did not want to end my journey this way and live with a defeated feeling for the rest of my life. I decided to continue for a doctorate degree. I switched to education for the study, as I had no courage to continue suffering the alienation for four more years. I applied to study in the Reading and Writing Instruction program at the University of New Hampshire.

With many fears and wonders I came to this program. When I had the first meeting with my new professors and peers, I found I bumped into another "Alice in Wonderland." This program was formed by a community of well-established fine writers. Among my peers, there were poets, fiction writers, people who had already published books, and even a former president of National Writing Center Association. I was an ESL student and a newcomer to the culture, who still struggled to understand others and express myself in English. I was sure that I was accepted into this program by mistake. From the close and active interaction between the peers and professors, I sensed that there was no way for me to hide and remain silent all the way through as I had done in the two-year English program. Soon my ignorance as a reader and writer in this Western world would be found out. Then I would be "deported," with a typical polite Western apology in a firm tone. Holding my breath, I started the program.

When I went to the first reading class, I was all prepared to hear book discussions with a "Formalist" view or "Deconstructionist" tone, or talks about sexual images and symbolism. Surprisingly, the professor started the class by reading a story and invited the class to share our connections with the story or our identification with the characters. Instead of giving us reading assignments, she asked us to make our own reading list. In the class, we read, talked and wrote not like English majors, but as real people did in life. The first time in so long, I left the class with a kind of fulfillment and joy.

During each reading discussion in this class, we shared our understanding and feelings about the reading. We made the connection between the world in the text and reality, we identified with the characters and experiences portrayed in the novels. We also questioned and argued with the authors and texts. In short, we reacted to the reading like real people with feelings and emotion, we used everyday language rather than a special discourse, we discussed the meaning of the text as well as the ways the meaning was constructed. Not only could I understand everyone in the class, but I identified with their connections and sharing. I felt I was not an outsider but a reader like anyone else in the class. Instead of being silent and hiding myself in the corner, I joined the interaction of the class and many times voluntarily shared my response to the reading.

With the same anxiety, I went to my first writing class, as I was not sure what kind of tone and language I had to borrow to get through this course. In the literature courses, I had *Cliff Notes*. For this course I might have to find new references. Writing like a doctorate student, I assumed, I might have to sound like Marx or Dewey. Interestingly, the professor started the class by asking us each to tell a story, a childhood story, such as "Fire in the House." He told his own story first, with a personal, intimate and nostalgic tone. One by one we told ours. I never thought I had a story, especially the one about fire in the house. I was intrigued by the others' stories. Theirs reminded me of my childhood, my life on the farm and the growing experiences in the unheated cement apartment buildings in China. I told my story:

In China, in the area where I lived, we didn't have fire place like you have here with chimney on the roof. We don't have central heat neither. When it was cold, we just put more clothes on. In winter, we dressed a lot no matter when we were outside or inside the house. We dressed our children with so much that they could barely walk. So they fell all the time. But as they were bundled with so much clothes on, when they fell down, they never hurt themselves, as their noses were at least two inches above from the ground. Of course they had hard time to get up too. When I was on the farm, in very, very cold days, each farmer would contribute a bundle of woods and get together in our little hut. They lit fire in the middle of our mud and straw-roofed house, like American Indians did in the woods. All the peasants in the village would come, chatting, smoking and making fun of each other around the fire. Sometimes we would kill a dog and eat it around the fire. We believe dog meat gives you most heat. That was the best time of the year.

The sharing of our memories and stories not only connected us, but set an intimate tone for the class. We shared, laughed, and learned about each other. My peers showed great interest in my story, as it was so different from others'. They kept asking me questions, and I kept talking and talking. Probably I said more in that one time than in two years in the whole English program. We wrote a lot in that class. In our writing, we told about our own experiences, discussed the things that interested or bothered us, and shared our observation and understanding of the world and life.

I was a different writer in the Reading and Writing program than I had been in the English program. In the latter one, I tried hard to sound like an English major in my writing. I imitated how the critics read and analyzed the text. Not only did I adopt their ways of reading a text, but I borrowed their terms and tone to discuss a text. A paragraph from my discussion of Willy, one of the main characters in Arthur Miller's *Death of a Salesman*, will give some insight:

Willy's situation exactly reflects this timeless universal problem. The sense of his modernness, I assume, is that his world is a modern one, so he has to wear modern clothes and display what is the most modern. Otherwise his tragedy can hardly bring about any pleasure of terror, pity and thought on the part of the modern audience. In essence, his dilemma is not different from Oedipus' and Hamlet's, and may actually be even worse in our modern world because man is more devalued than he was in Greek and Elizabethan ages.

Writing in the Reading and Writing program was different. The essential thing was to be yourself. Instead of relying heavily on outside references, I had to go deep inside myself, to find what I knew, and who I was. Instead of sounding like someone else, I had to sound like me in my writing. It was not easy at first. After two years of training in the English program, finally I thought I learned to sound like an English major with academic discourse and Western intellectual tone. Now I had to twist back to myself again, I did not know my own thought any more after giving them no value in the English study. In expressing this feeling, I wrote:

My maternal grandmother told me that it was excruciatingly painful when she had to relearn to walk with her unbound feet after they had been bound for months. At present, I am in a similar situation to my grandmother's in learning to write with my voice. After I have been trained to sound like somebody else for years in writing, I don't know my voice any more. It is like a faded memory, so distance, so strange and so vague. Did I have a voice of my own? Can I have it back? Am I deformed as a writer?

I was struggling for a while. Slowly my numb mind started to wake up and I gained consciousness by constant writing and sharing my own experiences, my own feelings and understanding of the things and people around me. I wrote not only academic papers, but also poems and stories, which surprised me, as I rarely wrote any stories and poems in my native language after I entered college. Here was one of the poems I tried first time in English:

A Woman Without a Name

My grandma never had a name.
When she was little,
She was called Daughter Number One.
When she was married,
She became Mrs So and So.
After she had children,
People called her the mother of the Zhang's house.

My grandma always wanted a name.
Once, she shook her mother's knees begging her:
"Mom, would you please give me a name?"
Slowly moving her head from her sewing, with a deep sigh,
Her mother answered her:
"Honey, I wish I could,
But girls are not supposed to have names."

My grandma always loved roses,
Especially, those red ones.
One night, her mom whispered into her ear
While she was asleep:
"Red Rose, oh, I wish I could call you,
My little Red Rose."

"Red Rose, oh, I would love that name,"
My grandma exclaimed with joy and regret,
When she heard what her mother called her
While she was asleep.
Red Rose, a name, my grandma always wanted,
But she was only called once by that name
In her sleep.

She lived for seventy-one years without a name.
At her tomb, we carved:

Red Rose Zhang
1880–1951

Though compared to my peers' my poems and stories sounded much more raw and childish, the experiences of writing them helped me discover something in me, understand risk-taking in learning and explore other ways to express myself.

I read and wrote all the time. As I did not have to pretend or to act like someone else, the reading and writing became easy and a joy for me. I could not stop. I did not just read and write for assignments, for grades, or for professors, but for myself. I found I had so much to say and express, and I had little difficulty in expressing myself in English. It was as if I went back to my farm life—no constraints, no deadlines, or any requirement—but just immersed myself in the reading and writing. By the end of the first semester, I read thirty-two books, twice as much as what I did in two years in the English program. I had written over two hundred pieces, in addition to a dozen research papers for the courses I took, more than I had ever written in the thirteen years since I first learned English.

In this learning community, people constantly shared reading, writing and thinking in classes, at research meetings or at any gatherings. At first I was not used to this interaction and openness in learning. Overwhelmed and confused with so much unfamiliarity, I sat silently through many classes and research meetings. My professors and peers did not leave me alone for too long, they poked me with all kinds of questions, starting with those about China, then moving to those about America. I spoke first in a whispering voice and timid tone: many people had to lean so much forward in order to hear me. Then with the encouragement of their interest and curiosity in whatever I said, my voice became louder and louder.

Instead of sitting there and feeling stupid, overwhelmed and confused with what I did not know, I began to ask questions. I started with questions like "What is 'lunch duty'?" "What is 'Basal'?" to "Why do you Americans have to worry about how students are evaluated? In China, this is the work of the authority. We teachers, simply teach, we even have no say about what textbooks we have to teach." "What's the relationship between students' self-evaluation and teaching?"

No matter what kind of questions I asked, I never sensed a slight hint by anyone that I was looked down upon as a person too ignorant to be one of them, which I was very much afraid of. My peers and professors never thought my questions were too trivial or naive, and always patiently answered my questions, enthusiastically discussed them with me, and showed great interest in my questions and ideas. Very often they were fascinated by the ways I phrased and expressed my ideas. They were seldom bothered by my accent, nonstandard English expressions and different metaphors and images. Instead they were amused by them and interpreted them as unique Oriental beauty and a different perspective. I was surprised by their recognition and discovery of something in me that I never gave any value to and even sometimes caused me to feel ashamed.

It is this recognition that invited me into the literate community which I felt no part of at the beginning, built my confidence as a learner and overcame my fear and feeling as an outsider. Through constant sharing and discussion about reading, writing and many issues of education and literacy with my peers and mentors, I understood more and more about American society, culture and people. In turn, this understanding helped me look at my native culture and world with different perspectives. My learning about the two worlds enlightened me and made me a reader, a writer and a thinker with much broader views than before. At any sharing time, I could not wait to share and express myself. My timid, uncertain and soft voice became loud, strong and passionate.

Interestingly, in the past when I tried hard to sound like others in my reading and writing, I alienated both myself and others. Now when I could just be me as a reader and writer, I came to know myself more and more, became closer to the people around me, and joined the community from which I thought I would always be excluded in this Western world. In this community, I grew as a writer with Oriental and Western integrated styles and a thinker with a view combining Marxism and pragmatism. Rather than hindering my learning and research, my Chinese cultural and formal academic training background became a strength and added a unique perspective to them.

My two very different learning experiences as a newcomer in this culture helped me understand the teaching of reading and writing. My former one alienated me as a learner and the latter one liberated me. My growing experiences as a literate person in the reading and writing instruction program made me realize that I was a reader and writer, different in many ways from many people in this culture. When I had difficulty understanding the others, or reading and thinking like my peers, it was not because of my low English language ability or my lack of knowledge of the Western world, but because of my different ways of reading the words and the world, and my different ways of expressing myself. Once I realized the beauty in my difference instead of denying myself and feeling inferior to others, I found my voice in reading and writing. I had the language and fluency to express myself in book discussion and writing. I could think, read, and write with power and imagination.

7

Recent Mexican Immigrants: Forgotten Voices in the High School Restructuring Process

Rosalie Giacchino-Baker

And there was a myth, a pervasive myth to the effect that if we only learned to speak English well—and particularly without an accent—we would be welcomed into the American fellowship. . . . The true test was not our speech, but rather our names and our appearance, for we would always have an accent, however perfect our pronunciation, however excellent our enunciation, however divine our diction. That accent would be heard in our pigmentation, our physiognomy, our names. We were, in short, the other.

—Madrid, 1988, p. 2

INTRODUCTION

Although meeting students' needs is the purpose of education, students' opinions are rarely sought or valued in the process of restructuring schools. Perhaps the most neglected student voices are those that speak languages and have cultures that educators do not understand; perhaps the most urgent voices are those of teenage immigrants who have only a few years to learn English and complete high school, the gateway to their future. We test English language learners (ELLs), grade them, label them, and track them based on their proficiency in English. By treating language minority students as products rather than participants in the educational process, we are doing nothing to stop the current cycle of failures. This chapter describes a study in which recent Mexican immigrants in an "English-only" California high school were asked to tell about their experiences in acquiring English, the key to their academic success and social acculturation. An important outcome of this study is a list of students' suggestions for restructuring their classrooms and school to provide inclusive and integrative programs for ELLs.

Participants reported that they were socially and academically alienated. They indicated a strong need to become part of campus activities and to become engaged in integrative learning, that is to say, education they could connect to the realities of their lives. They recognized that making some of these connections was their personal responsibility, but they also suggested ways their teachers, school, and school system could help them acquire English, make academic progress, and become a part of the campus community. This chapter proposes that these immigrant students' recommendations warrant attention in the restructuring process.

RATIONALE

Our secondary school classrooms are increasingly filled with students who immigrate to the United States as adolescents. Even though many of these students have been educated in their first languages, they find that their linguistic and educational achievements, as well as cultural identities, are negated as they begin the long path to learning English. They are commonly labeled limited English proficient (LEP) thereby proclaiming them deficient rather than encouraging their status as aspiring bilinguals.

Only a few recent studies have examined the complex problems in providing educational quality and equity for LEP students at the high school level (Lucas, Henze, & Donato, 1990; Minicucci & Olsen, 1991; Olsen, 1988; Tikunoff et al., 1991). The major accomplishment of this body of research has been to identify some of the features of schools that successfully promote the achievement of LEP students. None of these studies, however, attempted to view the linguistic and academic challenges on an American high school campus through the eyes of recent Mexican immigrants. It is from this unique perspective that my research was conducted.

BACKGROUND

Most secondary schools in California offer academic coursework only in English. They are commonly referred to as English-only schools to differentiate them from bilingual schools, which offer classes in students' first languages. Common practice in English-only schools is to place minority language students in programs that stress competence in English as a second language as a prerequisite for most classes. Since it can take from five to seven years for older learners to develop academic proficiency in a second language (Cummins, 1981; Krashen, Scarcella, & Long, 1982), students who have been educated in their first languages are often denied the opportunity of making academic progress at a pace with their English-speaking classmates. Some respond to the challenge by exceeding all expectations. Many become complacent about coursework and accept the lowered goals of tracking systems that keep them in less-demanding classes. Too many of them drop out of school.

According to the California State Department of Education (1992), LEP students now constitute 21.1 percent of the approximately five million students in California's public schools, from kindergarten through grade twelve. Almost 76 percent of all identified LEP students speak Spanish as their primary language. Statistics give a stark but depersonalized view of what happens to Latino students in the American educational system. According to the American Council on Education's *Ninth Annual Status Report on Minorities in Higher Education* released in January 1991, the number of Latino students finishing high school dropped from 60.1 percent in 1984 to 55.9 percent in 1989. By comparison, the number of Anglos getting their diplomas that year dropped slightly to 82.1 percent, while African Americans showed a small gain at 76.1 percent. Even those Latinos who finish high school are often unable to get into four-year colleges because of their inadequate academic backgrounds and their inability to communicate in standard English.

Recent Mexican immigrants function differently than other Latinos, even their Mexican American counterparts, in American school systems (Carter & Segura, 1979; Durán, 1983; Lucas et al. 1990; Matute-Bianchi, 1986; Suarez-Orozco, 1989; Trueba, 1989). These newly arrived students have the lowest college entry rate and the highest high school drop out rate of any group from a Spanish-speaking country.

DESCRIPTION OF THE STUDY

The research site, Capital High (a pseudonym), was a suburban high school in Southern California with 2,786 students, 49 percent of whom were Latino and 24 percent of whom had been identified as LEP. The programs for LEP students included three levels of English-as-a-second-language (ESL) classes and specially designed academic instruction in English (SDAIE) in some math, history, and science classes. The term SDAIE is used to describe instruction in which teachers attempt in some way to adapt lessons to the linguistic and cultural needs of LEP students. All classes, except foreign language classes, were taught in English.

The fourteen principal informants in this year-long study, eight males and six females aged fifteen to nineteen, were chosen as Mexican immigrant students who would have the greatest likelihood of success in an American school. Criteria for selecting them were based on nationality, length of stay in the United States, teacher recommendation, previous educational background, and English class attended. I selected Mexican students who had entered U.S. schools at the secondary level and whose teachers had recommended them based on demonstrated motivation and effort, not necessarily achievement. Since it was beyond the scope of this study to deal with the many Mexican immigrants who are illiterate in their first language, I also chose informants who had at least completed *la primaria,* elementary school, which students in Mexico attend for six years.

To establish a longitudinal view of participants' language experiences, the fourteen informants chosen for the study included four students in ESL 1 classes; three students in ESL 2 classes; three students in ESL 3 classes; and four former ESL students, one in each of the four tracks of the "regular" English program (remedial, basic, college preparatory, and honors) offered at Capital High.

In the report of this qualitative study, the terms "co-researcher" and "interviewee" are used interchangeably to refer to the fourteen principal informants. The term "co-researcher" is more accurate, since it better defines the pivotal roles these students played. They were not the subjects of this study. They told their stories and then reviewed and critiqued my analysis of their accounts. They established a bond with other co-researchers and described a responsibility they felt for the study as a microethnography, a focused description of their linguistic and cultural world on an American high school campus.

As the principal researcher, I used a variety of qualitative techniques to conduct this microethnography. I recorded and analyzed these fourteen students' accumulated reports of how they used and acquired English. Through semistructured interviews, I asked these Mexican students to describe their formal and informal language experiences, their help-seeking strategies, and their progress and problems in a multilingual, multicultural educational setting. I was a participant observer of their classes, between class breaks, pep rallies, lunch hours, and after-school activities, including sports events and Regional Occupational Program (ROP) training. I asked them, as co-researchers, to validate findings and make suggestions for improvement in their learning environments.

Research methodology included thirty-four audiotaped, semistructured interviews; thirty days (175 hours) of participant observations in classrooms with forty different teachers; and seventy-five hours of out-of-class participant observations during sixty-two visits to the research site over a one-year period. Spanish was used to communicate with all Mexican students. Students kept language logs of when and with whom they spoke English. Most of these entries were also in Spanish. Each of the fourteen co-researchers was interviewed (and audiotaped) at least twice, for periods of about fifty minutes, and "shadowed" for two complete school days. The first interview with each co-researcher took place prior to participant observations in classes. Followup interviews provided verification, correction, and clarification of initial interviews, participant observations, informal discussions, and English language logs.

Teachers, counselors, and on-site and district administrators were consulted formally and informally throughout the year-long study. These conversations took place in classrooms, teachers' lounges, administrative offices, and meetings. None of these discussions was audiotaped, but detailed notes were taken.

Research data included more than 900 pages of field notes and interview transcripts (translated into English) that were analyzed through the constant comparative method of data analysis as described in Bogdan and Biklen (1982) and Lincoln and Guba (1985). That is to say, I coded all incoming data with meaning indicators that were analyzed in the light of previously learned information through a system of unifying themes, categories, and properties organized in outline form. These organizational units expanded or contracted as their characteristics defined reality as seen through the eyes of the fourteen co-researchers. I noted possible relationships between categories and themes when making final analyses.

Co-researchers participated in all stages of data analysis, including a critique of the final report. Discussions with school personnel served to triangulate data from co-researchers. All raw and analyzed data were audited by two colleagues familiar with qualitative research techniques. The confidentiality of all students and school personnel who participated in this study was maintained through the use of pseudonyms.

FINDINGS

Two of the major themes that emerged from this study related to students' perceptions of the factors that affected their academic progress and to students' suggestions for educational changes. The following is a brief discussion of these two themes, based on co-researchers' experiences and supported by their statements. Page numbers refer to citations listed in Giacchino-Baker (1992) which is a complete report of the findings of this study. A short introduction of the co-researchers will precede a discussion of findings.

Co-Researchers in Context

Co-researchers came from geographical areas of Mexico that ranged from rural ranchos, to small towns, to Mexico City. Although eleven of them had studied English for at least two years as part of their normal curriculum in either the public or private junior high schools (*la secundaria*) in Mexico, none of them said they could understand or speak English when they arrived in the United States. Their experiences ranged from those of Samuel [ESL 1], a fisherman from an isolated village, who had never heard English, to those of Adriana ["post-ESL"], who had had daily contact with English in Tijuana.

All interviewees were highly motivated. It was maintaining their motivation that all co-researchers identified as a major challenge at Capital High. Each of the co-researchers described personal goals and family values as reasons to learn English. Their personal goals included a desire to speak English well, to become educated in the United States, to have more and better job choices, and to make money to help their families. All interviewees said that their families valued education and English, but eight of them admitted that their parents' need for financial assistance might interfere with their educational goals.

Co-researchers said their motivation became weaker and their efforts decreased as they worried about negligible improvement in learning English. Their confidence was undermined by their limited number of successful language experiences. Their self-esteems were deflated by perceived attitudes toward Mexicans.

The end of the students' first year was critical in terms of student motivation. Gabriel [ESL 2] admitted his ambitions were stifled by harsh realities when he said, "It's not what I want to be; it's what I can be" (p. 152).

Cecilia ["post-ESL"], who had been in California for three years, explained that few people expected much from her or her friends.

[We have to have] *ganas*, wanting to study and to show everyone that being Mexican does not mean we can't do it. A lot of people think that Mexicans don't know anything, but we can do it. We can show the world that we are better if we try. . . . If you want to, you can do things. (p. 263)

Cecilia's powerful statement identified her as a survivor of the school system. It reflected her understanding of cultural prejudices that overshadowed her daily struggles with language. Co-researchers' doubts about their ability to succeed in American society continued to be fueled, however, by their perceived lack of progress in English. Their motivation and efforts could not compensate for their lack of opportunities to understand and use English.

Although all co-researchers said they wanted to learn to speak English, they described very few situations in their neighborhoods, homes, and workplaces in which it was natural for them to use English. They expressed hesitancy about their ability to perform basic language functions in their community.

The large number of Spanish speakers in the area around Capital High made school the most reliable source of English speakers available to co-researchers. During their first two years at the high school, co-researchers had class schedules that often segregated them from English speakers. It wasn't until their junior year, long after most immigrant students drop out, that co-researchers talked about having contacts with English speakers.

Interviewees' comments about meeting Americans through extracurricular activities revolved around issues of access and language proficiency. Co-researchers were aware of the benefits of talking to English speakers, but they did not have access to them.

Co-researchers explained that they felt powerless in the face of institutionalized roadblocks on their paths to learning English, a key to academic progress. They discussed the following educational issues, many of which are often not limited to language minority students.

EDUCATIONAL AND INSTITUTIONAL FACTORS THAT AFFECT STUDENTS' USE AND ACQUISITION OF ENGLISH

An increasingly large influx of immigrants has strained Capital High's school district which, like many in California, is struggling to establish programs for ELLs. Co-researchers claimed to have problems learning English because of inappropriate class placements, class content, teaching methods, and teacher expectations.

Class Placements

Interviewees described many of their required and elective classes as unchallenging. Institutionalized placement procedures were based on English language proficiency, biased tracking systems, and placement tests that did not include ongoing evaluation of academic progress. Students became locked into certain class sequences in which they repeated coursework they had already completed in Mexico, as explained by Gabriel, who scored poorly on his initial math placement test because he was so nervous:

This class [general math] is . . . too easy for me [makes a groaning noise]. . . . When I arrived at this school, they gave me a math test, and I didn't do well. . . . That's why they placed me in a low class. In Mexico I was already almost in the high group where we had to use letters with formulas, in algebra already. . . . She [the teacher] knows. . . . I think they will change me to algebra at the semester. (p. 215)

Unfortunately, Gabriel's teacher did not allow him to take algebra the following semester. Most other co-researchers were also advised to take business mathematics and consumer mathematics rather than prealgebra or algebra. Their frustrations echoed those of a Central American refugee quoted by Suarez-Orozco (1989): "I'm not a crab; I don't want to go backwards" (p. 130). Placements in unchallenging classes affected students' motivation and self-esteem and undermined their future educational goals.

Class Content

Co-researchers at all levels of English proficiency were concerned about a lack of connection between their personal or cultural experiences and the school curriculum. They were frustrated by the fact that most teachers paid no attention to their interests or needs. Gabriel was one of three interviewees who responded positively to a teacher who tried to make these connections:

What that class has is that it teaches us history through the present. We can say to him [teacher], for example, *¿Qué significa esta palabra?* . . . He gives us examples about ourselves, of what happened in history. He uses us as examples. He explains everything. We talk. . . . Sometimes we make comparisons with Mexico, with its system of government. It's communication. I like it. (p. 220)

As noted by Freire and Macedo (1987), language involves both the word and the world. Most co-researchers reported that teachers did not try to help them make connections between classroom activities and daily realities. In a U.S. history class that I observed, for example, "vocabulary words" included "immigrant" and "prejudice," but the teacher did not elicit any student reactions to these terms, what Freire and Macedo termed "generative words." Interviewees' concerns are supported by second-language theories that posit that optimal language input should be interesting and/or relevant so that learners concentrate on meaning, not form.

Teaching Methods

Co-researchers at all levels depended on teachers to present lessons they could understand and to help them understand, speak, read, and write English better. They gave examples of effective and ineffective teaching methods in their ESL classes, their specially designed academic classes, and their regular content-area classes. In all their classes they were frustrated by a lack of integrated English language support, insufficient use of collaborative learning, and lack of primary language support.

Lack of Integrated English Language Support (Listening, Speaking, Reading, and Writing)

Co-researchers at all levels said they could understand lessons more easily if teachers used a variety of verbal and nonverbal cues to help them. They were able to pinpoint helpful language modification techniques such as repeating, paraphrasing, and simplifying language, as well as speaking loudly, clearly, and at a reasonable rate of speed. They were aware of how teachers used visual aids such as those Genoveva described in her ESL 1 class:

We learn in a way that isn't boring. . . . I understand what is happening. . . . She tries to explain to us with her hands so that we understand her, or she draws for us so we know what the word is . . . [and] she teaches with objects, pointing to what it is. (p. 224)

Co-researchers explained that they could not function academically if reading was the primary instructional strategy, as was the case in many classes at Capital High. Weak reading skills were of major concern to students, especially those in ESL 3 and "regular" English classes who were often faced with challenging reading assignments in compacted course loads the year before graduation. They talked of receiving little help from content-area teachers, whom they described as unaware of their reading problems in a second language. They reported no coordination between the literacy requirements for their English classes and their academic classes. Only Ramón ("post-ESL") talked about teachers who "helped him get the meaning out" of his readings (p. 135). Often under time pressures, co-researchers explained that they needed but did not get teachers' help as they struggled with technical vocabulary as well as basic comprehension. Cecilia's reaction to reading *The Scarlet Letter* was typical: "There are words that I don't understand . . . when I'm reading I don't get much out of it" (p. 134). They explained that they often resorted to copying passages directly from books because they did not understand them well enough to express their own ideas.

The writing problems related by twelve out of fourteen interviewees were confined to mechanics: handwriting, spelling, punctuation, and grammar. Yolanda (ESL 2) said she could not find mistakes in her own work before teachers make corrections: "I write them [words] like I think they're correct, but afterwards I see that some are right and some are wrong" (p. 137). Bárbara (ESL 3) said teachers gave her no writing help in her academic classes.

Two students expressed other types of writing concerns. Gabriel (ESL 2) stated that he wanted teachers to assign writing topics that were important and useful. Ramón ("post-ESL") indicated that he appreciated guidance from his teachers in how to organize his writing and adapt it for different audiences. He specified that he needed to know "what the teacher is asking for in the assignments" (p. 139).

Interviewees explained that there was very little need to speak English in any of their classes. Few teachers engaged students in an type of oral interactions in English, especially collaborative learning.

Insufficient Use of Collaborative Learning

Consistent with the findings of Kagan (1986), thirteen of fourteen interviewees reported that they would consult classmates before going to teachers for academic help. Co-researchers indicated that teaching methods needed to include more small-group activities. Antonio said that collaborative work in his biology class taught through specially designed academic instruction was very helpful for learning the scientific concepts.

He puts us to work. He explains it on the board, and we do it in groups. There are four of us. . . . When we were looking at cells . . . he gave us a microscope to look in to see vegetable and animal cells. Then he had us draw them and discuss them. You learn like that. (p. 231)

Unfortunately, small-group work and hands-on learning were more consistently reported in advanced classes. Beginning students who would have profited equally and possibly more from collaborative and experiential learning were usually left to read the book and answer the questions at the end of the chapter.

Lack of Primary Language Support

Most teachers expected students to work directly in English without any assistance or collaboration. A few allowed them to discuss lessons in Spanish. Unfortunately, none of their teachers *encouraged* students to make the transition to English after establishing conceptual understanding in Spanish. Once the concepts were understood, it would have been easier for students to express them in English as explained by Cummins (1983) in his common underlying proficiency theory (CUP).

Language choice was an aspect of teaching methods that provoked heated comments by co-researchers. All of them, except Ramón, the honors student, stated that they were often frustrated by their inability to ask or answer questions in English. Gabriel [ESL 2] explained:

Sometimes it's better to have a teacher who speaks Spanish. . . . If I have a question in biology class and the teacher doesn't speak Spanish and we can't ask the question in English or if he doesn't understand us in English, our questions remain unanswered. (p. 245)

Interviewees identified a need to speak Spanish with bilingual teachers: "Speaking Spanish with the teacher . . . is more for identification. We identify more with the teacher when we speak our own language" (p. 246).

Interviewees were unanimous, however, in stating that teachers' respect for students and their languages, insistence on high academic and classroom discipline standards, and teaching skills are most important to students' success.

TEACHERS' EXPECTATIONS

Co-researchers said teachers' academic and personal support made it easier for motivated students and offered possibly the only lifeline for students whose motivation, *ganas*, was lacking. Cecilia ["post-ESL"], a strong student, explained how her school life had changed because her teacher convinced her that she belonged in a college preparatory class rather than a remedial class:

> Mrs. Thompson, who used to be my ESL teacher last year, asked me which English class I had, and I told her I had remedial. She asked me, "Why do you have remedial? If you want to, you can have college prep." I said to her, "Isn't it real hard?" and she said, "No, I think you can do it." She's the one who convinced me that I could do it. . . . There are some really nice teachers who understand you. They say, "You can." And well, you move ahead. (p. 216)

Interviewees said they could always tell whether their teachers cared about their learning. Ramón, the only co-researcher in honors classes, tried to articulate the difference between teachers' expectations in his regular classes and in his honors classes:

> This year I made a very drastic change coming from . . . regular classes to the most difficult ones that this school offers. I am learning a lot. The change is extraordinary. . . . [In regular classes] you really don't have to think. You just have to put down the facts that they give you. It's totally different, totally. (p. 235)

Although the distinctions described by Ramón apply to honors classes in general, they are especially evident in the perceptions many teachers have of language minority students. Statements similar to the following one, made by a social studies teacher, were made by many of the teachers I consulted at Capital High:

They follow everything we do exactly in the book. They would be lost if we did a thematic approach like the new social studies framework recommends. They couldn't handle it. Many of them are not very bright. (p. 237)

Teachers' attitudes, therefore, were influential in determining how well students understood lessons, how comfortable they were asking and answering questions, and how they perceived themselves as learners. With placement procedures, class content, and teaching methods, they constitute the major educational and institutional factors determining students' use and acquisition of English for both social purposes and academic purposes.

Co-researchers were able and willing to offer many suggestions to the challenges facing their teachers and school.

STUDENTS' SUGGESTIONS FOR RESTRUCTURING THEIR SCHOOL EXPERIENCES

An analysis of factors that affected interviewees' lack of linguistic and academic progress reveals a consistent lack of integrative education. Interviewees expressed a profound sense of isolation in their academic and social experiences on an American high school campus. All of their suggestions for improvement involved the need to make connections. They recognized that making some of these connections are their personal responsibilities, but they also suggested changes that their teachers and school and school system can make:

Integrative Suggestions for Students

- Students should actively look for ways to use English in and out of class.
- Students should request classes that match their academic background (not their ability to function in English).
- Students should take pride in their linguistic and cultural heritages while trying to become comfortable with the English language and American customs.

Integrative Suggestions for Teachers

- Teachers should relate curriculum to students' needs, interests, and previous knowledge.

- Teachers should help students understand lessons by using teaching methods and materials that are appropriate for second language learners.

- Teachers should encourage student interaction through the use of collaborative learning.

- All teachers should respect students' first languages and encourage them to be used to support and clarify academic instruction.

- Teachers should have high academic and behavioral expectations for all students.

Integrative Suggestions for Schools and School Systems

- Schools should make immigrants feel like a welcome part of the student body.

- Schools should provide classes and programs that support students' English language needs and give them opportunities to interact with native English speakers.

- Schools should provide students and teachers with educational materials that are appropriate for second-language learners.

- Schools should remove the remedial stigma now attached to ESL classes and academic classes taught through specially designed academic instruction.

- Schools should provide equal access to extracurricular activities and should involve students in organizing additional activities to meet their social, academic, and linguistic needs.

- Schools should provide special counseling services about educational programs, opportunities, and financial assistance available to language minority students.

- Schools should provide open channels of communication for all students and their families.

CONCLUSION

The education of language minority students is a politically and emotionally charged issue. Perhaps skills in standard English are not enough to remove the prejudicial stigma of "other" that American society assigns to certain groups, including African Americans, Mexican Americans, and Native Americans. Perhaps, as suggested by Madrid (1988), the questionable ideal of an "accentless" society will not ensure equality. It would be naïve to assume that any common language could erase decades of prejudice. It is reasonable, however, to propose that schools must be structured so that students can develop their ability to function in standard English while establishing a bicultural identity. Bilingual and bicultural competencies increase the possibility of students' access to institutions of social and economic power that themselves must be changed to reflect the needs of our pluralistic society.

The voices of recent immigrants should not be forgotten in the process of restructuring our high schools. These students have expressed an urgent need for making connections between their educational past and present, between the languages and cultures of their school and family, and between their economic past and future. The findings of this study reflect the realities experienced by fourteen unique individuals, but I hope they will contribute to the dialogue that values students' opinions in the planning, implementing, and assessing of future educational programs. As stated by Trueba (1987), "The ultimate test of micro ethnography as a useful research tool in educational research will be its capacity to impact the reality and the quality of the educational process" (p. v).

REFERENCES

American Council on Education. (1991). *Ninth annual status report on minorities in higher education.*

Bogdan, R., & Biklen, S. (1982). *Qualitative research for education.* Boston: Allyn & Bacon.

California State Department of Education. (1992). *Language census report for California public schools. 1992.* Sacramento: California State Department of Education.

Carter, R., & Segura, R. (1979). *Mexican Americans in schools: A decade of change.* New York: College Entrance Examination Board.

Cummins, J. (1981). Age on arrival and immigrant second language learning in Canada: A reassessment. *Applied Linguistics, 2,* 132–149.

Cummins, J. (1983). The role of primary language development in promoting educational success for language minority students. In California State Department of Education, Office of Bilingual Education (Ed.), *Schooling and language minority students: A theoretical framework.* Los Angeles: California State University, Los Angeles.

Durán, R. (1983). *Hispanics' education and background: Predictors of college achievement.* New York: College Entrance Examination Board.

Freire, P., & Macedo D. (1987). *Literacy: Reading the word and the world.* South Hadley, MA: Bergin & Harvey.

Giacchino-Baker, R. (1992). *Recent Mexican immigrant students' opinions of their use and acquisition of English as a second language in an "English-only" American high school: A qualitative study.* Unpublished doctoral dissertation, The Claremont Graduate School, Claremont, CA.

Kagan, S. (1986). Cooperative learning and sociocultural factors in schooling. In California State Department of Education (Ed.), *Beyond language: Social and cultural factors in schooling language minority students.* Los Angeles: California State University, Los Angeles.

Krashen, S., Scarcella, R., & Long, M. (Eds.). (1982). *Child-adult differences in second language acquisition.* Rowley, MA: Newbury House.

Lincoln, Y., & Guba, E. (1985). *Naturalistic inquiry.* Newbury Park, CA: Sage Publications.

Lucas, T., Henze, R., & Donato, R. (1990). Promoting the success of Latino language-minority students: An exploratory study of six high schools. *Harvard Educational Review, 60*(3), 315–340.

Madrid, A. (1988, March). *Diversity and its discontents.* Paper presented at the Fourth Annual Tomás Rivera Lecture, 1988, National Conference of the American Association for Higher Education, Washington, DC.

Matute-Bianchi, M. (1986). Ethnic identities and patterns of school success and failure among Mexican-descent and Japanese-American students in a California high school: An ethnographic analysis. *American Journal of Education, 95,* 233–255.

Minicucci, C., & Olsen, L. (1991). *An exploratory study of secondary LEP programs. Vol. 5 of series: Meeting the challenge of language diversity: an evaluation of programs for pupils with limited proficiency in English.* Berkeley, CA: BW Associates.

Olsen, L. (1988). *Crossing the schoolhouse border: Immigrant students and the California public schools.* San Francisco, CA: A California Tomorrow Report.

Suarez-Orozco, M. (1989). *Central American refugees and U.S. high schools: A psychosocial study of motivation and achievement.* Stanford, CA: Stanford University Press.

Tikunoff, W., Ward. B., Romero, M., Lucas, T., Katz, A., van Broekhuizen, L., & Castaneda, L. (1991, April). Addressing the instructional needs of the limited English proficient student: Results of the exemplary SAIP descriptive study. Symposium conducted at the American Educational Research Association, Chicago.

Trueba, H. (1987). *Success or failure: Learning and the language minority student.* New York: Newbury House.

Trueba, H. (1989). *Raising silent voices: Educating the linguistic minorities for the 21st century*. Cambridge, MA: Newbury House.

8

Restructuring as an Integrative Process

Sam Crowell and Renate Caine

INTRODUCTION

As always, it seems that the effectiveness of public schools is at the center of our political and social debates. Recent years have seen the ebb and flow of numerous reform efforts aimed at increasing student performance and identifying "world class" standards. Amidst these demands for higher standards of excellence is the recognition that there is a need for an education that prepares students for the challenges of a complex, diverse, and changing society. The Secretary of Education in 1992 stated that "for the first time in our history, we are called upon to educate all youngsters and to prepare them to live and work in a world transformed by new technologies, demographic shifts, and economic globalization." We live in a world of transition and change. Fundamental shifts in the nature of knowledge and the nature of institutions are occurring. There is the implication that schools as we know them are not adequately meeting this challenge and that substantive restructuring at all levels is required. Consider the following statements by Secretary Riley. "The traditional organization of schools . . . is inadequate to the new conditions of American life." "American educators must now aim to prove that excellence and equity are not in conflict." "Our teacher education institutions must transform themselves, in order to support the kind of learning that new teachers must engage in." The transition is pervasive. Its effects are systemic. It is not a matter of doing what we do better, rather; we must rethink the very nature of our purpose.

We have observed the latest wave of restructuring reform with great interest and anticipation. We have worked with state agencies, districts, and individual schools. Although we have seen promising ideas, approaches, and innovative designs emerge, we have to agree with Jesse Goodman (1995) that in most instances educators have failed to ask important and substantive questions about the purposes of education, the nature of learning, and how schooling fits into the larger social and political context. Second, we have also observed that most often there is no theoretical understanding for the multiplicity of programs operating at a school site, resulting in confusion about their work, mixed expectations, and fragmented efforts. Third, and most important, is the erroneous assumption that change is external and targeted at instrumental objectives. This is consistent with schools' emphasis on learning as observed behavior, but it fails to recognize that substantive change is an internal process requiring individual and social transformation. We will argue that substantive change emerges from a process of dialogue, inquiry, and reflection. Restructuring results from the collective community of teachers, staff, administrators, parents, and students who are allowed to give voice to their work, questions, and creative ideas. In an atmosphere of trust and support not only do schools become different places but individual lives are transformed both professionally and personally.

This chapter is a brief account of our experience with several schools in which a process of change occurred within an active discourse community and resulted in a positive transformation of a school culture. One school has been featured on national television and continues its ongoing transition both structurally and foundationally. In another school the transformation began as one discourse community, and the positive results are enticing others to form similar discourse groups. In this chapter we try to understand the implementation of the change process in terms of complexity theory and from a "reconstructive" postmodern perspective. Finally, we offer a critique of most reform processes and suggest an alternative basis for ongoing change.

SOME GUIDING ASSUMPTIONS

The authors, and our colleague Geoffrey Caine, agreed to assist Dry Creek Elementary School in their process of restructuring. A Title I school located in a rural suburb north of Sacramento, California, Dry Creek represented a rather unexceptional school with a wide disparity of teaching expertise. Its teachers, however, as most teachers we know, were dedicated to their students and to making a positive difference in their students' lives. The principal, Cindy Tucker, was recently appointed to the school and had created a leadership partnership with her resource teacher, Kris Halverson. The school expressed great interest in creating a school environment based on recent understandings of the brain synthesized in Renate and Geoffrey Caine's book *Making Connections: Teaching and the Human Brain* (1991).

We began the change process with what we feel were several important assumptions. Some were hunches based on our previous experiences with change. Others were more grounded in our emerging understanding of systems theory. Our first assumption was that substantive change takes time. We therefore agreed on a minimum association of five years. Second, we felt strongly that there is no single picture of how a school should look and that if there is a strong unifying theory guiding them, a school will self-organize according to its particular context, needs, and history. Decisions about what they become are their decisions, not ours. Our third assumption was that restructuring involves a relationship among everyone at the school and that custodians, secretaries, attendance clerks, resource specialists, and cafeteria workers as well as teachers would begin to perceive their roles as connected to a unity of purpose and may be open to redefinition. Everyone would participate and have an equal voice. The fourth assumption was that restructuring is a process, not a product, and emerges out of substantive and ongoing dialogue. The particular outcome of structure and function is a manifestation of the quality of these processes and must continually change as individuals and groups grow in their awareness.

A COMMITMENT TO DIALOGUE AND PROCESS

Restructuring began at Dry Creek Elementary School when all members of the school agreed to meet in mixed-role groups two hours a week to talk about the purposes of learning, the nature of schooling, the relationships in the school that supported their work, and the personal fears and hurdles they experienced. There was no grant, no rich budget, no goals, no expectations of change, no coercion—just a dialogue process designed to internalize some understandings of learning, to ask questions, and to explore ideas and values. Everyone participated two hours a week on their own time!

The groups met informally, often in individual homes, and with a few organizational rules. Each person had begun reading a process book called *Mindshifts* (Caine, Caine, & Crowell, 1994) to help provide a general focus. Any interactive discussion was preceded by an invitation for each person to share thoughts, feelings, experiences, and ideas without interruption or debate.

The initial disgruntlement of finding two additional hours in an already busy schedule turned into an unexpected community of trust and bonding. When we revisited the school several months later and suggested that the composition of the groups might change, we were met with wide resistance. The discourse groups had become an essential part of their lives. Questions and insights were authentic responses to their work and their thinking. Dialogue volleyed back and forth from deeply personal beliefs and experiences to an examination of social conditions, mores, and expectations. Discussion about their work began to change from a discussion of methodology to a broader conception of educational practice.

THEORY-DRIVEN PRACTICE

What had not been apparent to the teachers and staff was that the contextual environment of their classrooms and school embedded all kinds of theoretical assumptions. When they began to examine these, they found inconsistencies that were not reconcilable with the values they were affirming. On their own they began to raise issues that implied changes in the school and classrooms. For example, flowers and plants became abundant throughout the school; music became an integral part of the environment; students were exposed to an atmosphere of listening and kindness that was different from a few weeks past. In some classes, students were given greater voice in decision making and the curriculum became more fluid and experiential. There was a different sense of collaboration and respect.

Over time, and with additional processing in groups and with us, the school began to exercise the power of their own voice in shifting the structures that seemed inconsistent with their growing awareness. The support staff decided to create a professional quality museum about the narratives of their own lives. They asked a museum curator to assist them in creating a theme, gathering artifacts, and interpreting the significance of their own life stories. These stories developed into an impressive format of case artifacts, narrative, and pictorial display. Students were trained to be curators by these same custodians, clerks, and secretaries, and these individuals became real and distinct apart from their social and institutional roles. The museum represented an enormous affirmation of distinctive human beings whose lives had a story to tell. The pride in this affirmation pervaded the entire school.

Critical issues, as felt by the faculty and staff, placed increasing burden on the previous school structures and slowly changes made their way into the organizational climate, instructional program, and curriculum. It is interesting to note that when tension and dissatisfaction surfaced at its worse, the school had abandoned the discourse groups in order to address some new district goal or demand. They had become work groups rather than a community that inquired into their basic ideas and experiences. Personal and social growth that had led to natural transformations were replaced by technical rationality and goal-directed change. These groups represented the more frequently observed technical-rational discussions usually held in schools—those kinds of meetings that react to some externally generated requirement or respond to a practical situation without regard to a larger context of issues. Technical-rational discussions are considered practical and to the point, but they serve to limit authentic inquiry and separate individuals from a sense of self-efficacy and purpose. These meetings served only to increase the tension and created a feeling of being overwhelmed and not in control.

Almost as soon as the faculty and staff returned to process groups, they took charge of the events that had been governing their time and efforts. They returned to consider issues in terms of the theory that was guiding their school. They also discovered that new issues of structure and organization as well as relationships had emerged that needed to be addressed. These issues were not insignificant. Although many things had changed throughout the school, they had maintained a rather traditional organizational structure. Some teachers had ventured farther than others, and natural partnerships emerged from common interests. Once tentative teachers began to assert their imagination and develop new organizational configurations that were more consistent with their emerging vision. Teachers at different stages of development continued to support one another and allow individual diversity to blossom while remaining committed to a common theory of action.

CHANGE AS AN INTERNAL PROCESS

This change process is still underway, and new narratives are created everyday. Those teachers who operate consciously from a theory of practice claim they would have to resign if they were forced to go back to being a mere technician. Those who are still struggling to integrate theory and practice seem to understand that their development is more perceptual than technical, and they continue to embrace a conscious process of "coming to be."

Perhaps this is the most profound discovery that we have made. Teachers and administrators may share a common language of pedagogical knowledge, use that language, and even implement it technically, but yet be far removed from its realization at an authentic level of practice. This is particularly true if the pedagogical approach represents a more holistic and integrative response to the educational context. Until the basic assumptions and mental models are perceived differently, we remain within a fixed ontology that permits a limited response to the educational environment. This response is made up of the perceptual commitments inherent in a fixed worldview.

Much attention has been given to differing epistemologies, and we do not want to minimize the excellent contributions that this sociology of knowledge has made to our understanding of ideology and social theories of action. What we would like to add to the discussion is the need for an "action ontology" that we believe lies at the heart of substantive and enduring change. The question of "being" goes beyond a given epistemology and encompasses our assumptions, values, and perceptions as they relate to our practice. Methodologies do not exist in a vacuum. They are context driven and embed an array of hidden assumptions. Assumptions about the nature of "time," "control," "authority," and "curriculum origination," for example, as well as about "instruction" and "learning," are dynamically related to classroom practice. A co-constructed curriculum that emerges out of investigation and dialogue among students and teachers may seem incomprehensible to teachers who view curriculum as an authoritative document that one must follow with little deviation. Abilities to "let go" or to "flow with the process" are not translatable into predetermined behaviors; rather, they reflect an ontology, an awareness of what one must "be" in order to "do."

Thus, more open epistemologies reflect an entirely different ontological response than those that exist within a closed system model embedding modernist assumptions of technical-rationality. As educational practice continues to be reconceptualized, its changes will require a greater emphasis on internal transformations rather than external instructions. Suzi Gablik (1991), who writes of transitions in art and culture, states that "the way to prepare the ground for a new paradigm is to make changes in one's own life" (p. 8). Restructuring, in this view, thus becomes an internal process of integration rather than any single set of external modifiers or organizational changes.

The role of the external is to support the process of internal change and to allow those changes to manifest themselves in ever new structures and functions. Change in this view becomes an authentic expression of emerging insights and is grounded upon a theory of action that combines personal and social transformational processes.

RESTRUCTURING FROM A POSTMODERN PERSPECTIVE

Guiding the change process through dialogue and discourse is a critical element that invites and allows a school community to inquire into their experience, assumptions, and beliefs. If beliefs and assumptions become mere clichés and certainties, however, a group can remain entrapped in various facets of a single perspective. When it is shown that modernist foundations cannot speak convincingly to issues of complexity, dynamism, or process, discourse groups begin openly to question the contradictions of previously taught theory and their lived experience. In addition, when they are provided with new possibilities to test and are invited to let new affirmations guide their thinking and practice, there is a sense of recognition and deep meaning that becomes a basis for a new kind of practice.

We use new understandings from twentieth-century science such as quantum theory, complexity theory, chaos theory, open systems theory, and neurosciences to begin to demythologize modernist practice. As we draw these into a philosophical context, using the sciences tends to legitimate the deconstructive process as well as provide an atmosphere where ideas can be openly tested. In addition, it serves to radicalize our previous notions of science and ironically to bring into question the very materialism on which it is based.

Although this desconstructive process is useful, it is nonetheless incomplete in providing an intellectual or experiential foundation for restructuring. We engage in what David Griffin (1988) and William Doll (1993) term "reconstructive postmodernism." Suzi Gablik (1991) has a number of statements that capture the essence of this perspective better than any single summary.

Reconstructivists are trying to make the transition from Eurocentric, patriarchal thinking and the "dominator" model of culture toward an aesthetics of interconnectedness, social responsibility and ecological attunement. (p. 22)

The holistic paradigm is bringing inner and outer—subjective and objective—worlds closer together. When this perception of a unified field is applied to human society and to culture, it makes us a codetermining factor in the reality-producing process. (p. 22)

If "world making" is the principal function of mind, then social reality does not just "happen" in the world but is constructed from the way our private beliefs and intentions merge with those of others. (p. 22)

Whereas the struggle of modernism was to delineate self from other, in the emerging realm of quantum inseparability, the world becomes a place of interaction and connection, and things derive their being by mutual dependence. (p. 150)

These statements suggest an emerging conception of relationship, interconnectedness, and a complex holism that is largely unexplored in our social institutions. It resists a deep-hearted cynicism while refusing to offer a naïve utopia. Further, it provides a foundation to ask questions in a different way and address a new set of practical issues. Postmodernism is not viewed solely as an absurd relativism; rather, it is perceived as infinite possibility. It allows for an iterative process to begin that we believe lies at the heart of transformation and makes possible sustained and substantive change. It is this deep and sustaining change that interests us most. We believe that this kind of change is at once personal, social, and spiritual, in that it has ramifications beyond classroom practice. A unitive consciousness develops that manifests itself in the outlook, decisions, and creative energy of individuals and organizations. Maxine Greene (1988) uses the term "wide-awakeness." Ellen Langer (1989) writes of "mindfulness." It is this sense conscious awareness and purposefulness that opens us to new questions and directions for educational practice.

BRAIN-BASED LEARNING

It is within this context that we offer the term "brain-based learning." *Making Connections: Teaching and the Human Brain* (Caine & Caine, 1991) synthesized much of the research on the brain that has developed during the past decade from the neurosciences, stress management, and optimal performance literature. Part of the hope of this book was to validate many of the humanistic educational practices in terms of new information about learning and the brain. It was to offer a counterpoint to the fragmentation that is so pervasive in schools and institutions. It was to point to the possibility of personal integration and to the vast potential of human learning that lies untapped. Brain-based learning is a way to synthesize complex research for educators and to provide legitimacy to the broader public. This has assisted us in working with teachers, administrators, and communities. It has provided us with a technical language that has, at its core, much broader implications. The following offers a brief summary of some of the important elements of brain-based learning.

LEARNING IS PHYSIOLOGICAL

One of the important findings of brain research is that learning is both physiological and mental. We have tended to focus separately on the brain rather than understand that the brain is part of a physical system that operates as a whole. The brain is part of a vast neuronal network that works in relation to our nervous system, chemical processes, and emotional states. Learning is as natural as breathing, but it can be inhibited or facilitated. Neuron growth, nourishment, and interactions are integral to the perception and interpretation of experiences (Diamond, 1985). Stress and threat affect the brain differently than do peace, challenge, boredom, happiness, and contentment (Ornstein & Sobel, 1987).

Everything that affects our physiological functioning affects our capacity to learn. Also, habits and beliefs are physiologically entrenched and therefore resistant or slow to change once they become part of the personality. Learning is more than mental ability and mental processing.

LEARNING IS EXPERIENTIAL

For a long time educational psychologists have emphasized an activity oriented curriculum. What is different here is that the nature of experience is broadened. Much of human learning is about making sense of experience. It may be an immediate experience, or it may be more autobiographical. Our experience may be bound up in cultural definitions, or it may be lacking contextual meanings to make it significant. Experience may be imagined or real; it doesn't matter to the brain, for the results are the same. The way we perceive and construct our experience is individual, social, and interactive.

In addition, the brain seeks patterns. It is the patterns of experience that have the most impact on our learning. As learners we need time to recognize, distinguish between, and consolidate multiple patterns. We need to process experiences in multiple ways to begin to see complex patterns and understand their interconnections. For this reason, dialogical approaches to learning and self-reflective processes offer powerful and alternative ways to understand experience and to participate in the social construction of knowledge.

LEARNING IS RELATIONAL

The attributes of community, trust, interaction, and shared discourse are consistent with what we know about the connective nature of the brain. Physiologically, the brain operates optimally in nonthreatening circumstances and when patterns of experience can be applied to real-life situations. Thus, when we create learning environments that emphasize positive, supportive human relationships and where individuals feel a sense of belonging, the conditions for substantive learning are increased. Moreover, when students have the opportunity to work together with others, there is an enhanced opportunity to process multiple experiences at the same time. This kind of purposeful social interaction and the application of learned content to real-life experiences help the brain connect to previous learnings.

Beyond the physiological, however, students can be helped to realize that the world itself is essentially relational and that the quality of those relationships is important for continued growth and understanding. If nothing exists outside of relationship, then events, defining qualities, identity, and the nature of experience itself require us to give attention to the kinds of relationships that are established. This opens us to different kinds of questions and to new possibilities of content.

Finally, relational learning means that content is always contextual. As the context of information is explored, the learner inevitably goes beyond that information and creates an understanding of the world. When we give attention to understanding the nature of context, we begin to realize the complexity of our connectedness and how those connections are often perceptual in nature and influence our responses to the world.

LEARNING IS NONLINEAR AND IS A
SELF-ORGANIZING PROCESS

Most learning does not take place in sequential order along some arbitrary continuum. Learning is always unique to individual processing. Because neural connections and individual experience patterns can never be predicted, all learning is chaotic and to some degree random. It is also intensely personal. There can be no such thing as removing the "personal" from learning. Yet in many instances we try to approach instruction with dispassionate objectivity. Once we recognize that learning, as well as all experience, is co-created with the world, we open ourselves to a different kind of educational discourse.

In addition, we learn through a process of self-organization. The brain must organize the complex web of information into patterns that make sense in a given context. In effect, the brain brings order to the complexity of our experience. The assumptions that we bring to our experience assist in this process. That is one reason that changing our assumptions can result in incredible personal changes. For once the rules of organization shift, information as well as our experience is organized differently.

Importantly, the nonlinear and self-organizing nature of the brain requires time to examine and explore itself as it organizes new information. Learning, therefore, is self-referential and needs ongoing processes that build upon reflection and dialogue. This self-referential quality can be applied to communities, social groups, societies, and cultures as learning is interpreted within broader contexts of meaning.

LEARNING IS MEANING-CENTERED

The brain seeks to create meaning. It processes in order to understand. Brain-based learning emphasizes that "surface knowledge" is the least meaningful kind of knowledge and that viewing learners as mere information processors denies us the full range of our humanity. If we begin to own the information we learn, to respond to it in personal ways, to participate in personal and social implications of that information, then we are beginning to create layers of meaning. These layers can include an investigation of knowledge itself and the coercive nature of its categories. Such layers can include cultural perspectives of knowledge that raise questions of legitimacy and power. Other layers may indeed be personal in terms of choices, goals, and aspirations and may be active and political or may take the form of the artistic and creative. Brain-based learning suggests that as surface knowledge moves to technical knowing to deep meaning, learning shifts from knowing to being. It suggests that the disciplinary divisions begin to dissolve at this level and insights from one discipline have relevance to others. In other words, the levels of connectedness become more and more obvious, knowing and being begin to merge as well.

This, of course, moves beyond physiology to philosophy, however, these understandings seem to us to be implicit not only in research on the brain but in the new sciences in general. Brain research is very compatible with questions arising from the areas of quantum physics and chaos and complexity theory, as well as other forms of research in complex, adaptive systems. We believe questions of transformation, emergence, self-reference, reciprocity, and nonmaterialistic reality are legitimate issues arising from this research which provides us with a different lens from which to view the world and moves us into creative response to questions of what it means to be human.

Brain-based learning, therefore, is not a set of instructional techniques or some new methodology; it is meant to provide a different way of viewing the nature of learning and to redefine learning in terms of our humanity. Although it makes use of materialistic notions of the brain and specific application of those understandings, it views these as limitations and seeks to place what we know about the brain within the context of integrating human experience with the realization of our inherent connectedness.

Brain-based learning became part of the reconstructive vision we explored with teachers. Their insights into their experiences and into the kind of humans we wish to become and the kind of human organizations we wish to help create became the focus of our common endeavor. As internal shifts manifested into classroom and organizational changes, we saw the value of trying to understand these transformations in a way that seemed consistent with the general approach we were taking. Complexity theory provided a path to these understandings.

COMPLEX SYSTEMS AND AN ANALYSIS OF CHANGE

We began this chapter with a description of the restructuring process, some guiding assumptions, and factors that we think led established discourse communities to alter their beliefs and assumptions and literally "become" different kinds of teachers and begin to create a different kind of school. We have also observed other schools achieve various levels of success and failure in the restructuring process. Throughout we have found the insights that emerge from some of the new sciences of complexity theory, chaos theory, and dynamic, complex systems to be most useful. In terms of its organizational implications the work of Margaret Wheatley in *Leadership and the New Sciences* (1994) is a wonderful introduction. The forthcoming book by Renate and Geoffrey Caine, *Education at the Edge of Possibility* (1997) examines more completely the nature of educational issues when viewed from the perspective of complex adaptive systems. In this chapter, however, we want to highlight three essential concepts that are crucial to understanding change from this point of view. They are self-organization, systemic co-evolution, and special attractors. Although self-organization was touched upon in the previous section, a slightly more technical description is beneficial.

Complex adaptive systems are present throughout the living world and are also part of many nonliving processes. These systems defy strictly mechanical explanations and instead tend to operate in an almost purposeful, "mind-of-their-own" fashion. Patterns of behavior are established, but they are changeable in how they are "perceived." These systems are highly interactive, dynamical, and always in process. They are part of a larger context and also help create that context at the same time. These kinds of systems are inherently creative and move in and out of chaos and order. Organizations of all kinds can be viewed as complex, adaptive systems. We are interested in understanding change from this perspective.

SELF-ORGANIZATION

Complex systems make substantive changes from an internal locus of control. Although external conditions may influence the need for a "decision" and the range of possibilities, the system fashions a unique and personal response to its conditions. What often precedes the movement into self-organization is what Nobel Prize winner Ilya Prigogine (Prigogine & Stengers, 1984) calls a "far-from-equilibrium state." This is characterized by conditions that offer multiple thresholds for decisions and in which the point of decision reaches a critical juncture. This is a bifurcation point, in which the system may form entropy or may create a new form of order out of the far-from-equilibrium state, or chaos.

To put this in everyday terms, it is out of a process of exploration and questioning that multiple possibilities present themselves. Once this occurs, we search for patterns that make the most sense to us and begin to converge toward a transitional "order." As William Doll (1993) states, "If cooperative, purposeful behavior (which leads to higher levels of organization) suddenly appears at critical threshold points, then teachers need to work toward finding these junctions in their own group interaction" (p. 105). This is what we observed happening in the discourse communities. The conversations, sharing, and discussions began, over time, to converge on ever more similar themes until individuals and the group decided on new possibilities to try. As the teachers embraced their acknowledged fears, they were supported by others branching out in similar yet unique ways. The constant process of diverging and converging represented the natural ebb and flow of chaos and self-organization. Doll suggests that this process may be the essential component of all deep and meaningful learning. Through self-organization a learning community can become a reality.

All complex adaptive systems self-organize. In the case of restructuring, organizations like schools can create processes that encourage and allow controlled chaos to occur and to invite choices that resonate with the context of the group. When the processes make possible a growing awareness of our assumptions, of learning theory, of the social context, then those choices are likely to reflect those understandings.

SYSTEMIC CO-EVOLUTION

One of the most interesting phenomena of complex, adaptive systems is the relationships among the various parts of the system and the simultaneous influence of the micro and macro elements upon each other. It was decided that the school as a whole would try to reflect the same kinds of values that each teacher was seeking to establish. So, for example, if teachers began to use music, art, and expressive kindness in their classrooms, then the office, cafeteria, and school grounds all incorporated those efforts as well. School meetings began with thoughtful or provocative quotations, genuine sharing, and reflection on practice rather than spending all the time on administrative details. These efforts at the macro level encouraged teachers and staff members at the micro level. Parents, community organizations, and district representatives were included in the process, creating a new kind of place with a new kind of practice. The emphasis, though, was on participating in a process, letting change emerge naturally from that participation.

Systemic co-evolution is the understanding that the parts and the whole reflect one another. Therefore, attention is given to the parts as well as the whole. Reflection consists of questioning how reflective each is of the other and the responsibility of each person in the process of reorganization. Obviously, this is not a smooth and even process, but the concept that the organizational structure must support and reflect the changes taking place is often not embraced. We have seen in many cases that teachers have been sent off to make changes in their classrooms while the administrative expectations and procedures actually contradict what the teachers are being asked to do. In other cases, an enlightened administration may make structural changes that are meant to assist teachers in new forms of thinking. Without processes that allow teachers and others to co-create similar environments, there is often a total lack of buy-in.

We believe that structural changes can prod teachers to consider a wider variety of options, but these changes need to be consistent with a unified vision and direction that is shared and that is part of a process of ongoing development. It is this third characteristic of complex adaptive systems that we want to address next.

SPECIAL ATTRACTORS

Special attractors are actually boundaries that allow patterns to replicate themselves in similar yet unique ways. For example, although every snowflake is distinctive, there is a boundary of patterns that makes each one identifiable as a snowflake. When complex systems undergo change, new pattern boundaries emerge from chaos that give definition to the self-organization taking place. These new patterns act almost like a magnet to help the system form a new identity. In a weather system, this may mean the difference between remaining a tropical storm or becoming a hurricane. In a school, it may mean a shift from a hierarchical organizational structure to a participatory one.

Understanding special attractors within an organizational context helps us appreciate the process of creating a field of vision that guides the choices we make and forms the basis of a new or modified identity. We have seen many schools change from one strategy to another or one program to another without having a foundation for the kinds of decisions that support that change. In other words, they may have realized that what they were doing was not working and that something new was being done somewhere else, and so they changed. The change did not alter their basic identity, however, nor did it result in any substantially new vision that would make subsequent decisions consistent. In most such cases, the change is merely external and does not significantly influence the nature of the schooling process. There has not been a redefinition of the organization that has been internalized and that may serve as a new basis for its environment.

We have found that when schools create a new identity for themselves the new self-concept begins to guide everything they do. When this identity has a foundation in both theory and practice, it can become part of the creativity within an organization. When this identity has its roots in an exploration of our humanity and with a commitment to become the persons we envision, then it has the potential for sustained inward transformation where a new kind of dialogue can take place.

RESTRUCTURING AS AN INTEGRATIVE PROCESS

The purpose of this chapter has been to emphasize that the quality of school restructuring is related to our ability to be part of an ongoing process of reflection and self-awareness. As our questions turn inward, we are faced with the contradictions of our behaviors, our institutions, and our society. We are brought into relation with others in a community of discourse to examine the implications of our questions, assumptions, and practices. And we are allowed to create changes that are consistent with our insights and abilities.

This process is made stronger when we have a basis for a reconstructive practice that addresses the very roots of our humanity and our inherent connectedness to the universe. These understandings contribute to an environment of renewal and meaning.

Finally, we become part of the creative process that does not fear or resist change, but perceives it within a context of our own transformation and as a natural extension of our being.

REFERENCES

Caine, G., Caine, R. N., & Crowell, S. (1994). *Mindshifts: A Brain-based Approach to School Restructuring*. Tucson, AZ: Zephyr Press.

Caine, R. N., & Caine, G. (1991). *Making Connections: Teaching and the Human Brain*. Washington, DC: ASCD.

Caine, R. N., & Caine, G. (1997). *Education at the Edge of Possibility*. Washington, DC: ASCD.

Diamond, M. C. (1985). *Brain Growth in Response to Experience*. Seminar, University of California, Riverside, March 23, 1985.

Doll, W. E. (1993). *A Postmodern Perspective on Curriculum*. New York: Teachers College Press.

Gablik, S. (1991). *The Reenchantment of Art*. New York: Thames & Hudson.

Goodman, J. (1995). Change without difference: School restructuring in historical perspective. *Harvard Educational Review, 65*(1), 1–29.

Green, M. (1988). *The Dialectic of Freedom*. New York: Teachers College Press.

Griffin, D. (Ed.). (1988). *The Reenchantment of Science*. Albany, NY: SUNY Press.

Langer, E. (1989). *Mindfulness*. Reading, MA: Addison-Wesley.

Ornstein, R., & Sobel, D. (1987). *The Healing Brain: Breakthrough Discoveries in How the Brain Keeps Us Healthy*. New York: Simon & Schuster.

Prigogine, I., & Stengers, I. (1984). *Order out of Chaos: Man's New Dialogue with Nature*. New York: Bantam Books.

Wheatley, M. (1994). *Leadership and the New Sciences*. San Francisco: Berrett-Koehler.

Selected Bibliography

Aronowitz, S., & Giroux, H. (1985). *Education under Siege*. New York: Bergin & Garvey.

Belenky, M., Clinchy, B., Goldberger, N., & Tarule, J. (1986). *Women's Ways of Knowing: The Development of Self, Voice, and Mind*. New York: Basic Books.

Blair, B., & Caine, R. (Eds.). (1995). *Integrative Learning as a Pathway to Teaching Holism, Complexity, and Interconnectness*. Edwin Mellen Academic Press.

Bowers, C. (1987). *Elements of a Post-liberal Theory of Education*. New York: Teachers College Press.

Caine, R. N., & Caine, G. (1991). *Making Connections: Teaching and the Human Brain*. Washington, DC: ASCD.

Caine, R. N., & Caine, G. (1997). *Education on the Edge of Possibility*. Washington, DC: ASCD.

Caine, G., Caine, R. N., & Crowell, S. (1994). *Mindshifts: A Brain-based Approach to School Restructuring*. Tucson, AZ: Zephyr Press.

Doll, W. E. (1993). *A Postmodern Perspective on Curriculum*. New York: Teachers College Press.

Gablik, S. (1991). *The Reenchantment of Art*. New York: Thomas & Hudson.

Giroux, H. (1988). *School and the Struggle for Public Life*. Minneapolis: University of Minnesota Press.

Giroux, H., Penna, A., & Pinar, W. (1981). *Curriculum and Instruction*. Berkeley, CA: McCutchan.

Green, M. (1988). *The Dialectic of Freedom*. New York: Teachers College Press.

Griffin, D. (Ed.). (1988). *The Reenchantment of Science*. New York: State University of New York Press.

Caval, J. (1991). *History and Spirit: An Inquiry into the Philosophy of Liberation*. Boston: Beacon Press.

Noddings, N., & Shore, P. (1984). *Awakening the Inner Eye: Intuition in Education*. New York: Teachers College Press.

Oliver, D. (1989). *Education, Modernity and Fractured Meaning: Toward a Process Theory of Teaching and Learning*. New York: State University of New York Press.

Orr, D. (1993). *Ecological Literacy: Education and the Transition to a Postmodern World*. New York: State University of New York Press.

Index

About the Contributors

RENATE CAINE is a professor at California State University, San Bernardino. Her teaching focuses on humanistic approaches to educational psychology and curriculum. Her research explores brain-based learning-teaching and integrative education. She, along with her husband Geoffrey, is the author of *Making Connections: Teaching and the Human Brain*.

ROBBIN D. CRABTREE is an assistant professor of communication studies at New Mexico State University where she teaches courses in international, intercultural, and development communication, and in qualitative research methods. Her research explores the nature of communication and social change in Nicaragua, El Salvador, Cuba, and India and along the U.S.–Mexico border.

SAM CROWELL is an associate professor at California State University, San Bernardino. His writing and research focus on reconceptualizing educational theory and practice. Currently his work examines the implications of the new science metaphors for education. His latest book, *The Reenchantment of Learning*, with Renate and Geoffrey Caine, will be published in Spring 1997.

SUSAN DRAKE is an associate professor in the graduate department of Brock University, St. Catherine, Ontario. Her teaching area is holistic education, and her research examines new models of education in changing times. She is particularly interested in collaboration as a model for work.

DANLING FU is an assistant professor in the College of Education, University of Florida. She teaches courses in language arts methods and supervises graduate interns in education. Her research interests focus on children's writing development. She is the author of *My Trouble Is My English*.

ROSALIE GIACCHINO-BAKER is an associate professor of education at California State University, San Bernardino, where she specializes in second-language and multicultural education. Her international experiences include work in France, Micronesia, England, Belize, Mexico, China, Thailand, and the Lao People's Democratic Republic. She has conducted research on issues related to Southeast Asian, Native American, and Latino students in California's schools.

TODD E. JENNINGS is an associate professor in the School of Education at California State University, San Bernardino. He teaches courses in developmental and educational psychology, research methods, and socio-cultural foundations of education. His research explores the developmental and educational foundations of social consciousness and human rights advocacy. He is currently Chair of the Department of Learning, Literacy, and Culture.

IVAN D. KOVACS is a professor of human development in the Department of Human Development at California State University, Hayward. Educated in Hungary, Dr. Kovacs has a background in clinical work. His current interests focus on interdisciplinary higher education and its related epistemological, personal, and group developmental issues.

DENNIS A. KREIL is the director of pupil services in the Placentia–Yorba Linda (Southern California) School District. He also serves as adjunct faculty at California State University, Long Beach. He writes in the areas of resiliency, motivation, and the changing roles of school psychologists.

BARBARA LARRIVEE is a professor of education in the School of Education at California State University, San Bernardino. Her research and writing explore effective teaching practices for students with learning and emotional problems as well as the challenges to other students identified as at risk of school failure. Her areas of specialization include teaching as social mediator, collaborative problem solving, developing student autonomy, and conflict resolution.

HELEN J. SHOEMAKER teaches in the interdisciplinary, undergraduate Department of Human Development at California State University, Hayward. She currently serves as the program advisor for returning student admittees of the Human Development Program for Adult College Education (P.A.C.E.). She is particularly interested in the role of advisors as co-learners in the process of critical reflection in the academic setting and the need for more participatory learning environments.

DUDLEY J. WIEST is an associate professor of educational counseling at California State University, San Bernardino. He is also in private practice as a psychologist working primarily with children with learning problems and their parents. His writing focuses on the areas of intrinsic motivation, postmodern approaches to child counseling, and children's spirituality.

ISBN 0-89789-496-0

EAN

HARDCOVER BAR CODE